COOKING NEW AMERICAN

COOKING NEW AMERICAN

How to Cook the Food You Love to Eat

The Taunton Press
Inspiration for hands-on living®

 The Taunton Press
Inspiration for hands-on living®

The Taunton Press, Inc.
63 South Main Street, PO Box 5506
Newtown, CT 06470-5506
e-mail: tp@taunton.com

Distributed by Publishers Group West

Editor: Joanne McAllister Smart
Layout: Carol Petro

LIBRARY OF CONGRESS CATALOGING-IN-PUBLICATION DATA

Cooking new American : how to cook the food you love to eat :
200 recipes from Fine cooking magazine / the editors of Fine cooking.
    p. cm.
 ISBN 1-56158-728-1
 1. Cookery, American. I. Taunton's fine cooking.
 TX715.C78422 2004
 641.5973—dc22

                                        2004009094

Printed in the United States of America
10 9 8 7 6 5 4 3 2 1

The following manufacturers/names appearing in *Cooking New American*
are trademarks: Nabisco®, Ocean Spray®

Acknowledgments

Special thanks to the authors, editors, art directors, copy editors, and other staff members of *Fine Cooking* who contributed to the development of this book.

Contents

Introduction

Over the ten years that we've published *Fine Cooking* magazine, we've had the privilege of working with the best cooks in America: top-notch chefs, cooking teachers, cookbook authors—experts who have shared their talent and fresh vision with our readership of passionate cooks. We've published thousands of their recipes and techniques, from which we've distilled this collection called *Cooking New American*.

Why "new American" and why this topic for our first book from *Fine Cooking*? Because we feel the recipes in this book are a perfect reflection of the way good home cooks like to cook today. This is a book you'll pick up over and over, whether you're looking for a quick answer to "what's for dinner tonight?" or you want to dream about what to serve at your next party.

By "new," we don't mean trendy, but rather fresh and contemporary, recipes for the kind of food you enjoy cooking and serving your family and friends. You'll find updated versions of American classics, simpler takes on international favorites, and exciting dishes that incorporate bold ingredients, like those we've borrowed from Italy but that are now so much a part of American cooking—balsamic vinegar, sun-dried tomatoes, and good imported parmesan, for example.

New American also embraces the seasonal vegetables, fruits, and herbs that we love to cook with and, of course, the cooking methods that deliver a lot of flavor fast, like sautéing and grilling.

Recipes are just half the story, however. From all our talented authors, we've learned the tricks and techniques that make the difference between a good dish and a great one, and we've woven that highly useful information throughout this book, with how-to photos, tip boxes, and lots of advice on working ahead, handling ingredients, and creating your own variations of recipes.

I know that my own copy of this book will soon be happily worn because, even though I have every issue of *Fine Cooking* magazine, I can find so many of the dishes I like to cook for my own friends and family together in *Cooking New American*. I think you'll use your copy in the same way, as a great resource to make all your cooking successful and delicious.

— MARTHA HOLMBERG,
PUBLISHER AND EDITOR-IN-CHIEF, *FINE COOKING* MAGAZINE

SMALL BITES

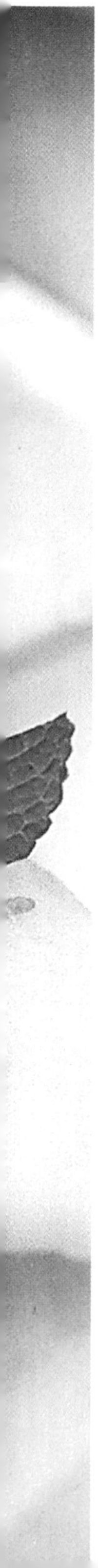

More relaxed—both in the preparing and the eating—than a formal sit-down first course, "small bites" are quite versatile. Alone, they are great appetizers for parties and dinners, but most can also be paired with a salad for a light and casual meal. Small bites, whether some prosciutto and marinated melon or fresh tuna pâté, are often enjoyed away from the actual dinner table—on a patio in nice weather, by the fire in the winter. And by making a few of these straightforward yet delicious recipes (many of which include make-ahead tips) you are on your way to hosting an inspired cocktail party.

THE RECIPES

Spicy Maple Walnuts

Marinated Goat Cheese with Bay Leaf & Peppercorns

Prosciutto with Marinated Melon

Frico

Peppered Shrimp

Hoisin Beef & Scallion Rolls

Fresh Tuna Pâté Scented with Rosemary

Bruschetta

Mushrooms with Sage, Parmesan & Prosciutto

Grilled Figs with Goat Cheese & Mint

Lemon-Pepper Cheese Coins

White Bean & Artichoke Dip with Pita Chips

Cheddar-Pecan Gougères

Sesame Parmesan Twists

Clams with Garlic-Butter Sauce

COOKING RIGHT

Start with the best nuts. Nut oils are very perishable so try to taste before you buy, and freeze them if you don't use them soon.

Check the nuts often. Nuts burn easily so be vigilant during toasting.

Taste and adjust seasonings. Once the nuts cool, taste them to see if they need additional seasoning.

Spicy Maple Walnuts

YIELDS 4 CUPS

These nuts continue to toast a bit from the intense heat of the glaze, so don't overbake them. Leave the ginger slices in the nut mixture for a delicious surprise. Pecans or hazelnuts are also great this way.

4 Tablespoons unsalted butter
⅓ cup pure maple syrup
6 quarter-size slices fresh ginger, halved
1 Tablespoon water
1 teaspoon ground ginger
1 teaspoon salt
¼ teaspoon Tabasco, or to taste
1 pound (4 cups) shelled walnuts

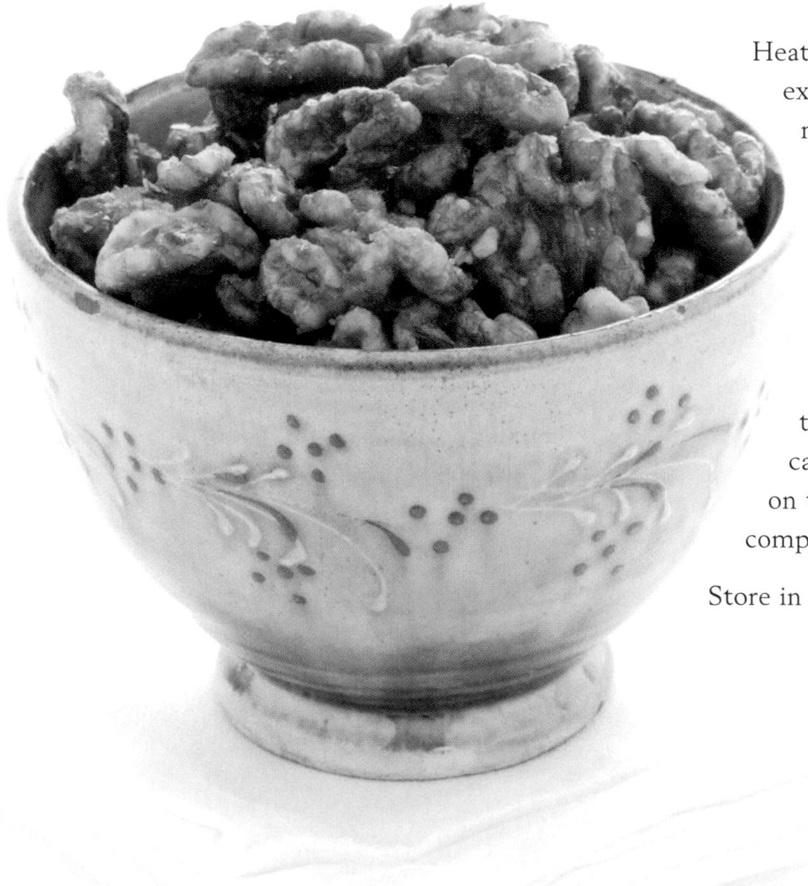

Heat the oven to 300°F. Combine all the ingredients except the nuts in a small saucepan and slowly simmer over low heat for 2 to 3 minutes. Put the nuts in a bowl, pour the glaze over them, and stir and toss to coat them with the glaze.

Line a baking sheet with foil and spread the nuts in a single layer on it. Bake for 30 to 40 minutes, stirring at 15-minute and then 10-minute intervals. When the nuts look light and almost dry as you toss them, they're done. Don't touch them; the caramelized sugar is extremely hot. Slide the nuts on the foil onto a cooling rack and let the nuts cool completely.

Store in airtight containers or plastic freezer bags.

—BARBARA J. WITT

MORE ROASTED NUTS

with foil and spread the nuts in a single layer on it. Bake for 30 minutes, stirring well every 10 minutes, until the nuts are deeply browned. Slide the nuts on the foil onto a cooling rack and let the nuts cool completely.

Store in airtight containers or plastic freezer bags.

Almonds with Parmesan, Rosemary & Fennel

YIELDS 3 CUPS

   Olive oil for the pan
1 Tablespoon chopped fresh rosemary leaves
2 teaspoons salt
1 teaspoon fennel seeds
¼ teaspoon freshly ground black pepper
2 egg whites
½ cup finely grated Parmesan
½ pound (1½ cups) blanched almonds
½ pound (1½ cups) skin-on almonds

Heat the oven to 300°F. Line a baking sheet with foil and spray or brush lightly with olive oil.

Grind the rosemary, salt, fennel, and pepper in a spice mill to a fine powder, or mince the rosemary

and grind the mixture in a mortar and pestle. In a large bowl, whisk the egg whites until they foam. Add the spices and cheese. Whisk again to combine. Add the nuts, stirring and tossing to thoroughly coat them. Spread them in a single layer on the foil-lined pan. Bake for 45 minutes, stirring every 15 minutes to redistribute the coating. The nuts will stick to the foil at first and need to be gently pried loose to expose them evenly to the heat. Slide the nuts on the foil onto a cooling rack and let the nuts cool completely.

Store in screw-top jars or airtight tins; plastic may cause the crisp coating to soften. ◆

Curried Pecans

YIELDS 4 CUPS

4 Tablespoons unsalted butter
2 Tablespoons canola oil
1 Tablespoon Madras curry powder
2 teaspoons salt
1 teaspoon ground cinnamon
¼ teaspoon ground cumin
¼ teaspoon cayenne
1 pound (4 cups) shelled pecans

Heat the oven to 300°F. Heat all the ingredients except the nuts in a small saucepan over medium heat to release the flavors and dissolve the salt. Pour the mixture into a large bowl and add the nuts. Toss and stir the nuts to coat them thoroughly. Line a baking sheet

Olives & Marinated Goat Cheese with Bay Leaf & Peppercorns

SERVES 4

Marinated goat cheese is a delectable topping for mixed greens. Use the marinating oil as part of a vinaigrette.

- 3 fresh or dried bay leaves
- 1 teaspoon white peppercorns, lightly crushed
- 1 teaspoon black peppercorns, lightly crushed
- ¾ cup extra-virgin olive oil; more as needed
- 2 logs goat cheese (4 ounces each), cut into ½-inch rounds with a warm, sharp knife
- 12 to 16 good-quality green olives in brine (such as Sicilian), drained
  Zest (in strips) from ½ orange
- 2 sprigs fresh thyme

In a small pan, combine the bay leaves, peppercorns, and olive oil and set over medium heat just until you begin to smell the bay leaves, about 3 minutes. Be careful that the leaves don't burn. Remove from the heat and let cool completely.

Meanwhile, sterilize a 16-ounce glass jar by rinsing it with boiling water, and dry it completely. Pour a little of the oil into the jar to cover the bottom and then add the goat cheese rounds and olives, spooning in the orange zest, thyme, bay leaves, and peppercorns to mingle around them. Pour in the rest of the olive oil, adding more straight from the bottle if needed to cover. Seal the jar and let marinate in the refrigerator for up to two weeks, checking every few days to make sure the cheese doesn't fall apart. (If it starts to disintegrate, use it right away.) Pull the jar out of the refrigerator about a half hour before serving. Don't eat the bay leaves.

—AMANDA HESSER

Prosciutto with Marinated Melon

SERVES 8 TO 10

A few simple additions transform a classic.

1 medium (4-pound) ripe
   honeydew melon (or any kind
   of melon except watermelon)
   Juice of ½ lime
½ teaspoon crushed red chile flakes
¼ teaspoon kosher salt
4 mint leaves, torn into small pieces
6 ounces paper-thin slices
   prosciutto di Parma
1 Tablespoon extra-virgin olive oil

Cut off the stem and blossom ends of the melon. Stand the melon on one cut end and slice off the remaining rind. Cut the melon in half lengthwise from stem to blossom end and scoop out the seeds. Halve each melon half, so that you have four long wedges. Slice the wedges crosswise about ¼ inch thick. Gently toss the melon in a bowl with the lime juice, chile flakes, salt, and half of the mint. Arrange on a platter, drape the prosciutto on top, and drizzle with the olive oil. Sprinkle with the remaining mint and serve immediately.

—CRAIG STOLL

HOW TO CHOOSE THE BEST MELON

Look for unblemished melons that are firm with no soft or bruised spots.

- **Lift it.** Compare the relative heft of the melons and pick the one that feels heaviest for its size.

- **Smell it.** Sniff thin-skinned melons at their base; a fragrance should be immediately noticeable even if faint.

- **Thump it.** Tap hard-skinned melons and listen for a hollow sound, not a dull thud.

Hoisin Beef & Scallion Rolls

YIELDS ABOUT 40 ROLLS

Hoisin sauce, which is used in Chinese cooking, is sweet, thick, and spicy. You'll find it with other Asian products in the supermarket.

- ½ cup soy sauce
- ½ cup vegetable oil; more for cooking
- 3 cloves garlic, crushed
- ½ cup chopped fresh ginger
  Freshly ground black pepper
- 1 pound London broil or flank steak, trimmed of fat
- ½ cup hoisin sauce
- 1 bunch scallions, white and pale green only, cut into 2-inch julienne strips

In a shallow dish, mix together the soy sauce, oil, garlic, ginger, and some pepper. Add the beef and marinate overnight in the refrigerator, turning once.

Heat the broiler. Pat the marinated meat dry and broil the steak, about 4 inches from the heat, until rare, 5 to 6 minutes per side. Cool completely and then slice very thin on the bias, across the grain of the meat. Trim the slices to form approximately 2x4-inch strips.

Brush a thin layer of hoisin sauce on each strip of beef. Lay a small bundle of scallion julienne at one end and roll up securely. Arrange on trays, seam side down, cover tightly with plastic wrap (make sure the plastic is in close contact with the beef), and refrigerate until time to serve.

—PAULA LEDUC

COOKING RIGHT

Freeze the cooked and cooled steak for about a half hour before slicing it, and it will slice more easily and neatly. Keep the layer of Hoisin sauce thin or it will ooze out the sides of the roll.

COOKING RIGHT

To smash garlic (and remove its skin), cover the clove with the flat side of a chef's knife and press down on it firmly, using the heel of your hand.

Fresh Tuna Pâté Scented with Rosemary

SERVES 6 TO 8

Lemon juice and fresh rosemary give the tuna a pine-citrusy zing. Served with a crisp white wine, or even Champagne, it makes a wonderful appetizer.

6 large sprigs fresh rosemary

2 teaspoons olive oil

8 ounces very fresh tuna

6 ounces (12 Tablespoons) unsalted butter, at room temperature

2 Tablespoons fresh lemon juice

Salt and freshly ground black pepper

Arrange the rosemary in an even layer in a nonstick skillet, add the oil, and heat over medium until the herbs are fragrant. Place the tuna on the rosemary branches and cook until the cooked white of the flesh has traveled about one third of the way up the side of the tuna steak, about 5 minutes. Turn the tuna over and cook until still quite pink inside, another 5 minutes. (The tuna will continue to cook as it cools.) Remove the tuna from the pan and allow it to cool. (Pull off any clinging herbs.)

In a food processor, combine the cooled tuna, the butter, lemon juice, salt, and pepper and process until smooth. Put the spread into a ramekin or small bowl, lightly cover the top with plastic wrap, and refrigerate until set. Grind more pepper over the top before serving with croutons or crackers.

—LISA HANAUER

COOKING RIGHT

Go slow when cooking the tuna to allow the rosemary to perfume the fish and to keep the meat supple. Overcooked tuna will make a dry pâté.

Bruschetta

SERVES 8 TO 10

If you are not in the mood for grilling (or the weather isn't cooperating), you can broil the bread slices to toast them.

1 1-pound loaf rustic country bread or crusty baguette, sliced ½ inch thick (cut baguettes on the diagonal) Extra-virgin olive oil as needed, about ½ cup
1 to 2 cloves garlic, peeled and halved (optional) Toppings (optional; see the recipes on the facing page)

Coat both sides of the bread with olive oil.

Light a charcoal fire and heat it until you can hold your hand above the grate for no more than 2 seconds or heat a gas grill to medium high. Grill the bread until one side has dark grill marks or is a deep golden brown all over and then turn to toast the other side. As soon as the slices are done, rub with the cut side of the garlic, if using, and drizzle with more oil, or add a topping. Cut into serving-size pieces and serve right away.

—TASHA PRYSI

Brush on olive oil. A light coating adds flavor and aids in toasting.

Heat the grill thoroughly. For nice grill marks like these, be sure the grate is well heated before the bread goes on.

Rub with cut garlic. For a depth of flavor, include this step with whichever topping you choose.

BRUSCHETTA TOPPINGS

Tomato, Garlic & Basil

YIELDS ABOUT 3 CUPS

1½ pounds ripe tomatoes (about 5), cut into ¼-inch dice
   Kosher salt
   Pinch cayenne
  1 clove garlic, mashed to a paste with a pinch of salt (use a mortar and pestle or a knife)
  ¼ cup extra-virgin olive oil
  2 leafy sprigs basil, leaves picked and torn or roughly chopped

Season the tomatoes well with salt and put them in a colander to drain for 5 to 10 minutes. Transfer the tomatoes to a bowl and fold in the cayenne, garlic paste, olive oil, and basil. Taste for seasoning and add salt or a pinch more cayenne.

Rustic Green Olive Tapenade

YIELDS ABOUT 2 CUPS

  1 clove garlic
  2 salt-packed anchovies, rinsed and filleted, or 4 oil-packed anchovy fillets

   Kosher salt
  ½ pound green olives, rinsed and pitted
  3 Tablespoons capers, rinsed well
  3 Tablespoons chopped fresh flat-leaf parsley
  ¼ cup extra-virgin olive oil
  2 hard-cooked eggs, peeled and roughly chopped

With a mortar and pestle, pound garlic and anchovies to a smooth paste with a pinch of salt. In a food processor, combine the olives and capers and pulse until the ingredients are roughly chopped. Transfer the mixture to a bowl and stir in the garlic-anchovy paste, parsley, olive oil, and eggs.

Fresh Ricotta, Mint, Lemon & Black Pepper

YIELDS ABOUT 1 CUP

 10 ounces fresh whole-milk ricotta (1⅓ cups)
  1 teaspoon finely grated lemon zest
   Kosher salt
  1 clove garlic (optional)
   Freshly ground black pepper
   Extra-virgin olive oil for drizzling
  1 or 2 sprigs mint, leaves picked and finely chopped

Combine the ricotta, lemon zest, and salt in a small bowl. Rub the grilled bread with garlic, if using, and spread the cheese mixture on top. Season with a few twists of pepper, drizzle with the olive oil, and scatter the mint on top.

Warm Herbed Goat Cheese

YIELDS ABOUT 1 CUP

  ½ pound fresh goat cheese, softened at room temperature
 2½ teaspoons finely chopped fresh thyme leaves plus 1 or 2 sprigs for garnish
  2 Tablespoons extra-virgin olive oil; more for drizzling
   Freshly ground black pepper

Heat the oven to 350°F. In a small bowl, stir the goat cheese, chopped thyme, and oil until blended. Spread the cheese mixture in an ovenproof ceramic crock or small gratin dish. Drizzle with a bit more olive oil and top with a few grinds of black pepper. Lay the thyme sprigs on top. Bake until the cheese is warm and creamy, about 10 minutes. Serve in the crock. ◆

Grilled Mushrooms with Sage, Parmesan & Prosciutto

SERVES 4 TO 6

Serve the mushrooms alone as hors d'oeuvres or with dressed mixed greens as part of a first course.

¼ cup freshly grated Parmesan
3 ounces prosciutto, sliced and chopped fine
1 teaspoon minced fresh sage, or ½ teaspoon crumbled dry sage
⅓ cup olive oil
   Juice of 1 lemon
1 pound small portabella, large shiitake, or large button mushrooms (or a combination), stemmed and wiped clean
   Salt and freshly ground black pepper
   Mixed salad greens (optional)

Combine the Parmesan, prosciutto, sage, and 2 tablespoons of the olive oil. Set aside. Combine the rest of the oil with the lemon juice and brush it on the mushrooms. Season them with salt and pepper.

Put the mushrooms, gill side down, on the grill over medium heat. Turn after about 3 to 4 minutes. Grill another 3 to 4 minutes until the juices begin to run and the mushrooms begin to soften. Move the mushrooms to the side of the grill. Spoon some of the Parmesan mixture into each mushroom. Cover the grill and let the mushrooms cook slowly for another 4 to 5 minutes until the cheese has melted slightly. Serve warm, alone as an hors d'oeuvre or on mixed greens as a first course.

—MOLLY STEVENS

COOK'S CHOICE

Portabellas or large shiitakes are ideal for this recipe, but good-size button mushrooms will also work well.

Bake the mushrooms instead of grilling. Heat the oven to 450°F. Start them gill side down on a baking sheet and follow the same cooking times and stuffing directions as in the recipe.

Grilled Figs with Goat Cheese & Mint

SERVES 4

Pancetta is cured (but not smoked) Italian bacon. Don't substitute American bacon: It takes too long to crisp on the grill.

½ cup (3½ to 4 ounces) soft fresh goat cheese

2 Tablespoons fresh breadcrumbs
   About 6 mint leaves, stacked, rolled into a cylinder, and cut into thin strips

1 Tablespoon finely chopped flat-leaf parsley
   Salt and freshly ground black pepper

12 fresh Mission figs

12 very thin (¹⁄₁₆ inch or less) slices pancetta

1 Tablespoon honey

½ teaspoon very finely chopped fresh thyme (optional)

Hollow the fig with your thumb and then add a teaspoon of the filling.

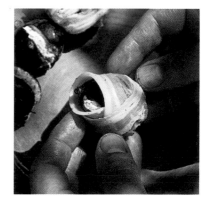

Wrap well but not too tightly. Very thinly sliced pancetta will crisp nicely just as the fruit softens.

In a small bowl, combine the goat cheese, breadcrumbs, mint, and parsley; season with salt and pepper. Cut the figs nearly in half length-wise, keeping them attached at the broad end. Hollow the center slightly with your thumb. Stuff each fig with about 1 teaspoon of the goat cheese mixture and squeeze very gently to close.

Wrap a slice of pancetta around each fig, overlapping with each revolution. Don't wrap the pancetta too tightly or you'll force the filling out or cause the figs to split. Cover the figs with plastic wrap and refrigerate (up to 1 day ahead) until ready to grill.

Grill the figs over a moderately hot fire to crisp the pancetta and to warm the figs and cheese, 8 to 10 minutes. Transfer the figs to a serving dish. Combine the honey and thyme, if using, and drizzle over the figs. Serve with good, crusty bread.

—BILL BRIWA

Lemon-Pepper Cheese Coins

YIELDS 6 TO 8 DOZEN

There are two ways to shape these savory crackers: Slice thin coins from a log of dough, or stamp out shapes with a cookie cutter. The log gives a more crumbly, crisp cracker, while the stamping method produces a lighter, flakier pastry.

6¾ ounces (1½ cups) all-purpose flour
¼ cup grated Parmesan
4 teaspoons grated lemon zest
1 Tablespoon coarsely cracked black pepper
1 teaspoon coarse salt
4 ounces (8 Tablespoons) unsalted butter, chilled and cut into small pieces
⅓ cup sour cream, chilled
1 large egg yolk
1 to 2 teaspoons fresh lemon juice, if needed

COOKING RIGHT

You'll get the lightest, finest zest— with the least amount of effort—if you use a rasp-style zester. Otherwise, use the small holes on a standard grater. Whichever kind you use, avoid getting any of the bitter white pith below the colored skin.

Combine the flour, cheese, lemon zest, pepper, and salt in a food processor. Process until combined. Add the butter and pulse until the dough resembles coarse crumbs. Add the sour cream and egg yolk and pulse again until just incorporated.

Test the dough by squeezing a bit between your fingertips—if it's too dry to hold together, sprinkle on a bit of lemon juice and pulse again. When the dough holds together, dump it onto a lightly floured surface and press into either a 12-inch log or a flat disk. Wrap in plastic and chill for 2 hours, or up to 2 days.

Heat the oven to 375°F. Slice the dough log into coins just under ¼ inch thick or roll the disk out to just under ⅛ inch thick and stamp out 1½- or 2-inch rounds or other shapes with a cookie cutter. Arrange them on an ungreased baking sheet and bake until well browned around the edges and no longer doughy in the center, 15 to 18 minutes for thinner coins, 20 to 22 minutes for thicker ones. Use a spatula to carefully transfer the coins to a cooling rack. The coins will keep in an airtight container for 2 days.

—MOLLY STEVENS

White Bean & Artichoke Dip with Pita Chips

SERVES 6 TO 8 AS AN APPETIZER; YIELDS ABOUT 2 CUPS OF DIP

Use plain, not marinated, artichokes for this artichoke dip.

- 4 pita rounds, 7 to 8 inches across, each sliced into 8 triangles, each triangle separated into 2 pieces
- 5 Tablespoons olive oil; more for drizzling
  A few pinches cayenne
  Kosher salt and freshly ground black pepper
- 1 can (15½ ounces) cannellini beans, drained and rinsed
- 1 can (14½ ounces) artichoke hearts, drained and rinsed
- 1 small clove garlic, chopped
- 2 Tablespoons fresh lemon juice
- 3 Tablespoons freshly grated Parmigiano Reggiano
- 1 teaspoon chopped fresh rosemary

Adjust an oven rack to the upper-middle position and heat the broiler to high. Toss the pita pieces with 3 tablespoons of the oil, a pinch of cayenne, and a generous amount of salt and pepper. Lay the pieces flat on two baking sheets. When the broiler is hot, put the pita pieces in the oven. After 2 minutes, flip them with tongs. Broil until crisp and browned, another 2 minutes. Turn off the broiler and let the chips sit for 2 minutes in the closed oven. Remove and let cool.

Meanwhile, in a food processor, blend the beans, artichoke hearts, garlic, and lemon juice to a smooth paste. With the machine running, add the remaining 2 tablespoons oil. If needed, add 1 to 2 tablespoons water to get a smooth consistency. Blend in the cheese and rosemary; season with salt and pepper. Transfer to a medium bowl, sprinkle with 2 generous pinches cayenne and drizzle with oil. Serve with the chips.

—TONY ROSENFELD

COOKING AHEAD

You can make both the chips and the dip a day in advance. Cool the chips completely and then store them in an airtight container. Cover the dip well and refrigerate it, but bring it to room temperature before serving for the best flavor.

Cheddar-Pecan Gougères

YIELDS ABOUT 4 DOZEN 2-INCH PUFFS

These irresistible cheese puffs are as fun to make as they are to serve. Beating the batter by hand can give you a feeling of accomplishment, but you can use an electric mixer if you would rather not get a workout.

1½ cups water

4 ounces (8 Tablespoons) unsalted butter, cut into 4 chunks

1 teaspoon kosher salt

Pinch cayenne

Pinch freshly grated nutmeg

7 ounces (1½ cups) all-purpose flour

6 large eggs, cracked into a small bowl, plus 1 more if needed

¾ cup chopped pecans, lightly toasted in a dry skillet

5 ounces grated very sharp Cheddar (about 1½ cups, lightly packed)

¼ cup finely grated Parmigiano Reggiano

Position racks in the top and middle of the oven and heat the oven to 425°F. Line two baking sheets with parchment.

In a medium heavy-based saucepan, heat the water, butter, salt, cayenne, and nutmeg over high, stirring to melt the butter. Bring to a boil and then dump in all the flour at once.

Take the pan off the heat and stir vigorously with a wooden spoon until you get a smooth, thick paste. Put the pan back on the stove, reduce the heat to low, and stir another minute or so to cook off more moisture. The dough should start to form a shiny ball and pull away from the sides and bottom of the pan.

When the dough is dry enough, take the pan off the heat. (Transfer to a stand mixer bowl now, if using.) Pour in 1 egg and then beat until it's well blended and the dough is smooth again. Repeat five more times

and then start to test the dough's consistency: It should fall from the spoon in a graceful "plop." If it seems too stiff, whisk up the last egg and add a bit of it and test again. (If you're using a stand mixer, use the paddle attachment. Use only low speed and don't overmix or the puffs will be tough.)

Add the pecans and Cheddar to the dough and carefully fold to distribute them. With a mini ice-cream scoop or two tablespoons, drop mounds about the size of a whole walnut shell onto the baking sheets, spaced about 1 inch apart. Sprinkle the shredded Parmigiano on top.

Bake in the heated oven until puffed, deep golden brown, and just barely moist inside, 25 to 30 minutes. (You'll have to break one open to really check the doneness.) Switch the positions of the baking sheets after 15 minutes for even baking. Transfer the gougères to a cooling rack. Repeat with any remaining dough. Serve when just barely warm or at room temperature.

—MARTHA HOLMBERG

1 The dough is ready for eggs when it starts to form a ball and pulls away from the sides and bottom of the pan.

2 Beating in the eggs takes a bit of muscle. At first the dough becomes exceedingly slippery and separated. (You might find it hard to believe it will ever come together again, but it will!)

3 A graceful strand falling from the spoon lets you know the batter is ready for shaping.

COOKING RIGHT

Thaw longer. Most packages of puff pastry recommend defrosting for 20 minutes—which never seems like enough. For pliable, workable sheets, try 35 to 40 minutes.

Blot moisture. If condensation creates beads of water, gently blot the dough with a paper towel before rolling and shaping.

Patch cracks. Check the seams where the dough was folded for packaging. If cracked, press the dough together with your finger as shown above.

Sesame Parmesan Twists

YIELDS 56 FIVE-INCH TWISTS

Frozen puff pastry is one of the few prepared products that delivers both convenience and quality, especially if you follow the tips suggested at left.

⅔ cup (about 2½ ounces) finely grated Parmigiano Reggiano
¼ cup (1-ounce jar) sesame seeds, lightly toasted
¼ teaspoon cayenne
¼ teaspoon chile powder
¼ teaspoon dried thyme leaves, crumbled
½ teaspoon kosher salt
2 sheets (about 18 ounces) frozen puff pastry, thawed
1 egg, beaten with a few drops water and a pinch of salt

Heat the oven to 425°F. In a small bowl, mix together the Parmigiano, sesame seeds, cayenne, chile powder, thyme, and salt. On a lightly floured surface, roll one of the pastry sheets to a 10x14-inch rectangle. Brush evenly with the egg wash and cut in half lengthwise to make two 5x14-inch strips. Distribute half of the cheese filling over one strip and lay the second strip on top, egg wash side down. Press the strips together with the rolling pin to fuse the two sheets. Cut the strip crosswise into 28 strips ½ inch wide. Lift a strip, twist it three times, and lay it on an ungreased baking sheet, pressing each end to keep the twists from unwinding during baking. Repeat with the second pastry sheet and the remaining filling.

Bake the twists until they're puffed, light brown, and dry looking throughout, 12 to 14 minutes. Test one by biting it to make sure it isn't doughy in the center.

Let the twists cool on a rack and serve as soon as they're cool, or within a couple of hours if possible.

—MARTHA HOLMBERG

Clams with Garlic-Butter Sauce

**YIELDS ABOUT 1½ CUPS SAUCE,
ENOUGH FOR AT LEAST 2 DOZEN CLAMS**

Garlicky-herb butter mingling with the clams' own juices creates a sauce that cries out for lots and lots of crusty bread for dipping.

5	ounces (10 Tablespoons) unsalted butter, at room temperature
12	cloves garlic
1	cup dry white wine
1½	teaspoons white-wine vinegar
2	Tablespoons heavy cream
	Salt and freshly ground black pepper
	Pinch cayenne
1½	teaspoons finely chopped fresh delicate herbs, such as flat-leaf parsley, basil, chives, or summer savory
2	dozen hardshell clams, oysters, or mussels, grilled or steamed

In a small skillet, melt 1 tablespoon of the butter. Add the garlic cloves and cook over low heat, tossing occasionally, until the garlic is golden and very tender, 25 to 35 minutes.

Remove the pan from the heat and let cool to room temperature. In a food processor, beat the remaining unsalted butter with the garlic mixture until nearly smooth; set aside.

In a small saucepan, bring the wine and vinegar to a rapid boil. Simmer to reduce the mixture by half and then whisk in the cream. Simmer to reduce this mixture to about ½ cup. Off the heat, whisk in the garlic butter, 1 tablespoon at a time, to produce a creamy emulsion. Season to taste with salt, pepper, and a judicious pinch of cayenne. Keep the sauce warm but avoid overheating, which will cause it to separate. Just before serving, stir in the chopped herbs. Spoon the sauce over grilled or steamed hardshell clams, oysters, or mussels. (For a prettier presentation, remove the top shell first.)

—SAM HAYWARD

COOKING RIGHT

Grill clams over a medium-hot fire for an added smoky flavor. To steam clams, heat them with a little water in a large lidded pot over high heat until they open.

SALADS

All of the recipes in this chapter feature the vivid flavors and the pleasing, often contrasting textures that we've come to expect and enjoy in today's salads. And that goes for the potato, chicken, seafood, and pasta salads you'll find here, too.

THE RECIPES

Arugula Salad with Nectarines & Fresh Raspberry Vinaigrette

Cherry Tomato, Mozzarella & Mint Salad

Asparagus & Blood Orange Salad

Roasted Red & Yellow Pepper Salad

Garden Lettuces with Baked Goat Cheese

Panzanella

Endive, Apple & Walnut Salad with Roquefort

Warm Potato Salad with Bacon & Apples

Grilled Potato Salad

Chinese Chicken Salad

Tuscan Grilled Chicken & Pepper Salad

Chicken-Mesclun Salad with Hazelnut Dressing

Updated Chef Salad

Sliced Salmon Salad with Olives & Tomatoes

Crab & Avocado Salad

Pasta Salad with Romesco Sauce & Roasted Red Peppers

Shrimp Bread Salad with Golden Garlic Vinaigrette

Arugula Salad with Nectarines & Fresh Raspberry Vinaigrette

SERVES 6

Substituting peaches for the nectarines also makes a tasty salad. You may have some leftover dressing, but it's delicious on other tossed green salads.

1   small shallot, minced
3   Tablespoons raspberry vinegar
½   teaspoon grated orange zest
1   Tablespoon fresh orange juice
    Kosher salt
2   ripe nectarines
6   Tablespoons extra-virgin olive oil
    Freshly ground black pepper
⅔   cup fresh raspberries
½   pound baby arugula or 1 pound arugula (about 4 small bunches),
    stems trimmed, thoroughly washed, dried, and torn into bite-size
    pieces (to yield about 8 cups, loosely packed)

Combine the minced shallot with the raspberry vinegar, the orange zest, half the orange juice, and a pinch of salt. Set aside.

Halve the nectarines, remove the pits, and then slice the halves into ¼-inch wedges; toss them with the remaining orange juice and set aside.

Gradually whisk the olive oil into the shallot and vinegar mixture and add a few grinds of black pepper. In a small bowl, very lightly mash the raspberries, allowing them to keep some of their original shape. Stir them gently into the vinaigrette.

Just before serving, put the arugula in a large bowl and toss with half the dressing to coat the leaves lightly. Toss the nectarines in 1 tablespoon of the vinaigrette. Arrange the arugula on a platter or individual dishes, topping the greens with the nectarine slices. Drizzle with a bit more dressing and serve.

—ALI EDWARDS

COOKING RIGHT

Since nothing wrecks a great salad quicker than a bite of grit, wash arugula—especially mature leaves—in a few changes of water. Taste a leaf before you make the salad to be sure you have gotten rid of any trapped sand.

Cherry Tomato, Mozzarella & Mint Salad

SERVES 6 TO 8

A fruity olive oil works really well in this summery salad.

1½ cups red cherry tomatoes (about 8 ounces)
1½ cups yellow cherry tomatoes (about 8 ounces)
¾   pound fresh mozzarella (use bocconcini or cut large balls into cubes)
    Kernels cut from 1 ear raw fresh corn (about ⅔ cup)
½   teaspoon salt
½   teaspoon freshly ground black pepper
¼   cup julienned fresh mint leaves
1   Tablespoon sherry vinegar
½   cup extra-virgin olive oil

Cut the cherry tomatoes in half, immediately putting them on a platter where their juices can collect. Scatter the mozzarella and the corn kernels over the tomatoes and sprinkle everything with salt and pepper; top with the mint. Drizzle with the vinegar and then with the olive oil. Toss gently.

—GEORGEANNE BRENNAN

COOK'S CHOICE

This salad looks pretty with a mix of small yellow and green cherry tomatoes, but you can also use larger tomatoes cut into wedges—and they can all be red.

COOKING RIGHT

To trim asparagus, snap the stalk with two hands; the tough part should break right off. For a cleaner look and less waste, cut off just the very bottom and peel the lower half of the stalk.

Asparagus & Blood Orange Salad
SERVES 4

Blood oranges look as dramatic as they are delicious, but you can use whatever oranges you have and the salad will still taste and look great.

    2   Tablespoons finely chopped shallot
    1   Tablespoon good-quality balsamic vinegar
    1   teaspoon sherry vinegar
    3   oranges, preferably blood oranges
    2 to 3 Tablespoons extra-virgin olive oil
 1½   pounds asparagus, trimmed
        Freshly ground black pepper (optional)

In a small bowl, combine the shallots with the vinegars and let the shallots macerate at least 20 minutes. Meanwhile, zest 1 of the oranges (avoid the white pith). Finely chop the zest and add it to the shallots.

Juice the orange to yield about ⅓ cup and add the juice to the shallots and vinegar. Slowly pour in the olive oil, stirring to mix.

Bring a pot of salted water to a boil. Add the asparagus and simmer until just tender, about 5 minutes. Drain, and spread the spears on paper towels to cool.

Cut off the ends of the remaining 2 oranges and peel them by running a sharp knife down the fruit vertically, following the contours. Slice the peeled orange horizontally into ¼-inch slices. Just before serving, toss the cooled asparagus with the vinaigrette. Arrange the spears and the orange slices on salad plates. Sprinkle with pepper, if you like, and serve immediately.

—SEEN LIPPERT

Roasted Red & Yellow Pepper Salad

SERVES 6

This is the time to pull out your best extra-virgin olive oil as there is little else flavoring the toasty peppers. If you can't find yellow peppers, use all red.

2 red bell peppers
2 yellow bell peppers
2 teaspoons red-wine vinegar
3 Tablespoons extra-virgin olive oil; more as needed
1 Tablespoon capers, rinsed and coarsely chopped
   Kosher salt and freshly ground black pepper
2 to 3 Tablespoons roughly chopped fresh flat-leaf parsley

Roast the peppers on a hot grill, over a gas burner, or on a baking sheet under the broiler, turning frequently, until blistered and charred all over. Put the hot peppers in a glass or metal bowl, cover tightly with plastic wrap, and let steam until cool enough to handle, 15 to 20 minutes. Slip the skins off the peppers with your hands.

Cut each cleaned pepper in half. Remove the seeds and stems and flatten the pepper. Cut the flesh into strips about 2 inches wide.

To serve, arrange the pepper strips on a serving platter; if you've refrigerated them, take them out an hour before serving. Whisk together the vinegar, 3 tablespoons of the oil, and the capers; season with salt and pepper. Pour the dressing over the peppers and scatter on the parsley. Serve immediately or let sit for an hour or two.

—MOLLY STEVENS

COOKING AHEAD

Once the peppers are peeled and cut into strips they can keep for a few days in the fridge. Drizzle a little olive oil on them first.

Garden Lettuces with Baked Goat Cheese

SERVES 8

Slices of breaded goat cheese transform a simple salad into something luscious. The warm cheese gently oozes over the greens while the crisped coating adds a welcome toasty texture.

3 small logs fresh goat cheese (12 to 14 ounces total)

½ cup extra-virgin olive oil; more as needed

3 to 4 sprigs fresh thyme
    About 1 cup fine fresh breadcrumbs

1 Tablespoon chopped fresh marjoram or thyme (or a mix of the two)

2 to 3 Tablespoons sherry vinegar or red-wine vinegar
    Salt and freshly ground black pepper

¾ pound garden lettuces: small oak leaf, red leaf, arugula, mâche, and any other tender lettuce greens, washed and dried well

Slice the goat cheese into 16 or more disks ½ inch thick. In a small dish, arrange the disks snugly and pour the olive oil over them (add more if needed to cover). Add the sprigs of thyme, cover with plastic, and marinate in the refrigerator for a few hours or overnight.

Heat the oven to 400°F. In a small bowl, mix the breadcrumbs with the marjoram or thyme. Remove the goat cheese from the marinade (reserving the oil) and coat with the breadcrumb mixture. Line a baking sheet with foil and put the cheese disks on it. Bake until the cheese is lightly bubbling and golden brown, 6 to 8 minutes.

In a small bowl, whisk the vinegar and ½ cup of the olive oil from the marinade. Taste for balance, adding more vinegar if necessary. Season with salt and pepper.

Toss the lettuces with the vinaigrette and arrange the greens on salad plates. On each mound of lettuce, lay two slices of goat cheese, browner side up.

—ALICE WATERS

COOKING RIGHT

Making your own fresh breadcrumbs is a snap. Simply grind up chunks of day-old bread in a food processor until they are the texture you want. Make more than you need and freeze the rest for the next time a recipe calls for fresh breadcrumbs.

Panzanella

SERVES 4 TO 6

Capers, celery, anchovies, hard-cooked eggs, and tuna are also delicious additions to this bread salad.

½ pound Italian bread, 3 to 4 days old, cut into 1-inch thick slices

½ cup cold water

1 medium cucumber, peeled, seeded, and cut into ½-inch cubes
   Kosher salt

¼ cup plus 1 Tablespoon red-wine vinegar

2 cloves garlic, minced

½ cup extra-virgin olive oil
   Freshly ground black pepper

1½ to 2 pounds ripe tomatoes (about 5), seeded and cut into ½-inch cubes

1 medium red onion (4 to 5 ounces), cut into ½-inch dice

½ cup loosely packed fresh basil leaves, torn

Sprinkle the bread with the water and let stand about 2 minutes. Gently squeeze the bread dry as you tear it into roughly 1-inch pieces. Spread the pieces of torn bread on paper towels to dry slightly, about 20 minutes.

Meanwhile, spread the cucumber pieces on a paper towel and sprinkle with salt. Let stand about 20 minutes to extract the bitter juices. Put the cucumbers in a strainer and rinse with cold water. Pat dry.

In a large mixing bowl, whisk together the vinegar, garlic, and olive oil. Season with salt and pepper to taste. Add the cucumbers, tomatoes, onions, torn basil, and the bread. Toss to combine and let stand until the bread has absorbed some of the vinaigrette, about 20 minutes.

—JOANNE WEIR

COOKING RIGHT

Reconstitute stale bread by sprinkling it with water. Gently squeeze out any excess water as you tear the bread into pieces. Don't be too zealous as you squeeze or the bread will fall apart.

COOKING RIGHT

For interesting endive shapes for the salad, slice the head on a sharp diagonal, turning as you go. Stop cutting when you get to the core.

Endive, Apple & Walnut Salad with Roquefort

SERVES 6

Wait to cut the endive just until before serving—like an apple, it browns quickly once cut.

1½ Tablespoons sherry vinegar
    Scant ½ teaspoon salt
¼ cup walnut oil
1 small handful watercress (1½ ounces) or flat-leaf parsley leaves
1 medium eating apple, such as Braeburn, Red Delicious, or Fuji
4 heads Belgian endive, wiped, brown leaves removed
3 ounces (¾ cup) walnuts, lightly toasted and crumbled
4 ounces Roquefort cheese
    Freshly ground black pepper

In a small bowl, combine the vinegar and salt; slowly whisk in the walnut oil. Put the watercress in a salad bowl. Quarter and core the apple, slice it ⅛ inch thick, and then cut the slices in half crosswise. Add the apple to the salad bowl. Slice the endive heads on a sharp diagonal into ¼-inch-wide strips, turning the heads as you slice and whittling down to the core. Add the endive to the salad, along with the walnuts. Toss the salad with the vinaigrette and arrange on plates. Crumble the Roquefort onto each serving, finish with a few grinds of black pepper, and serve.

—ALAN TANGREN

VIBRANT VINAIGRETTES

Try these on green salads as well as on grilled fish, seared steak, steamed green beans, and boiled potatoes. Whisk or shake the vinaigrette with your favorite tool and store it for up to a week in the refrigerator.

Spicy Ginger-Lime-Garlic Vinaigrette

YIELDS ABOUT ½ CUP

1 teaspoon finely minced fresh ginger
½ teaspoon finely grated lime zest
½ teaspoon minced garlic
¼ teaspoon Dijon mustard
¼ teaspoon table salt
⅛ teaspoon sugar
2 Tablespoons plus 2 teaspoons fresh lime juice
1 teaspoon white-wine vinegar
6 drops hot sauce, like Tabasco; more to taste
¼ cup grapeseed oil or other neutral-flavored oil

In a small bowl, whisk together the ginger, lime zest, garlic, mustard, salt, sugar, lime juice, vinegar, and hot sauce. Slowly whisk in the oil.

Garlic & Basil

YIELDS ABOUT ½ CUP

3 small garlic cloves, smashed and peeled
6 Tablespoons good-quality extra-virgin olive oil
14 fresh basil leaves
2 Tablespoons white-wine vinegar
1 teaspoon packed finely grated lemon zest
½ teaspoon Dijon mustard
¼ teaspoon table salt
⅛ teaspoon freshly ground black pepper

Put the garlic and oil in a small saucepan and heat to medium low, so the cloves are just barely sizzling but not browning. Simmer for 10 minutes, remove from the heat, and add 10 of the basil leaves. Let sit for about another 20 minutes and then remove the garlic and basil leaves.

In a small bowl, whisk together the vinegar, lemon zest, mustard, salt, and pepper. Slowly whisk in the flavored oil. Roll the remaining basil leaves into a tight roll and slice across to make thin shreds. Stir into the dressing.

Raspberry-Thyme

YIELDS ABOUT ½ CUP

2 Tablespoons white-wine vinegar
1 teaspoon balsamic vinegar
½ teaspoon chopped fresh thyme (or ¼ teaspoon dried)
½ teaspoon Dijon mustard
¼ teaspoon table salt
⅛ teaspoon freshly ground black pepper
6 to 8 fresh or thawed frozen raspberries
6 Tablespoons good-quality extra-virgin olive oil

In a small bowl, whisk together the white-wine vinegar, balsamic vinegar, thyme, mustard, salt, and pepper. Add the raspberries and crush them to a rough purée with a spoon or your whisk. Slowly whisk in the oil. ◆

—MARTHA HOLMBERG

COOKING RIGHT

Fold the potatoes gently to coat them evenly without breaking them up.

Warm Potato Salad with Bacon & Apples

SERVES 6; YIELDS ABOUT 5 CUPS

On the cool evenings of early and late summer, this salad staves off the chill. Seared chicken breasts, roasted pork loin, or ham are great accompaniments.

1½   pounds Yukon Gold potatoes, peeled, halved lengthwise, and sliced into ½-inch half-moons
¼   cup olive oil
     Kosher salt and freshly ground black pepper
3   thick or 4 regular slices bacon, cut into ½-inch pieces
½   cup diced yellow onion (¼-inch dice)
⅓   cup apple-cider vinegar (5% acidity)
1   sweet-tart apple (like Gala), peeled, cored, and cut into ¾-inch dice
1   Tablespoon chopped fresh flat-leaf parsley
1½   teaspoons chopped fresh rosemary

Heat the oven to 400°F. Put the potatoes in a large bowl and drizzle with 2 tablespoons of the oil. Season well with salt and pepper and toss.

Spread the potatoes on a large baking sheet and roast until they're slightly brown and easily pierced with a fork, 15 to 20 minutes. Meanwhile, heat the remaining 2 tablespoons oil in a large skillet over medium heat. Add the bacon and cook, stirring occasionally, until golden brown, about 10 minutes. Using a slotted spoon, transfer the bacon bits to a paper towel to drain. Add the onion to the pan, season with salt and pepper, and cook until the onion is softened, 3 to 4 minutes. Add the vinegar, mix well, and then add the cooked potatoes, apple, bacon, parsley, and rosemary. Gently fold everything together until evenly coated. Season with salt and pepper and serve immediately.

—DAVID PAGE AND BARBARA SHINN

Grilled Potato Salad

SERVES 4 TO 6

This salad is best made with truly new potatoes. If you can't find them, use larger red-skinned potatoes, but blanch them first in boiling water for a few minutes until barely fork-tender.

3 small red onions (about 1 pound total), cut into ½-inch rounds

2 Tablespoons olive oil; more as needed

1½ pounds baby new potatoes, halved (unless tiny)

2 teaspoons fresh thyme leaves
Salt and freshly ground black pepper

¼ cup mixed chopped fresh herbs (choose from parsley, tarragon, dill, chervil, basil, chives)

For the vinaigrette:

1 teaspoon Dijon mustard

3 Tablespoons white-wine vinegar

6 Tablespoons extra-virgin olive oil

Skewer the onion rounds with toothpicks to secure them. Brush the onions with olive oil and toss the potatoes with more oil, thyme, salt, and pepper. Slide the potatoes onto skewers. Grill the vegetables over medium-low heat for 15 to 20 minutes, turning occasionally, until the potatoes are browned on the outside and very tender inside and the onions are soft.

Meanwhile, whisk together the mustard, vinegar, salt, and pepper. Slowly whisk in the olive oil; taste and adjust seasonings.

When the vegetables are done, coarsely chop the onions and toss the onions and potatoes with the vinaigrette until coated, and then toss with the herbs. Taste and add more salt and pepper if necessary; serve warm.

—MOLLY STEVENS

COOKING RIGHT

To grill the onions for the salad, skewer them first. This will keep the rings together as you turn the slices. Remove the toothpicks before chopping.

Chinese Chicken Salad

SERVES 2 TO 3 AS A MAIN COURSE

COOKING AHEAD

You can make the dressing a day ahead. Keep it refrigerated, but let it come to room temperature before tossing it with the salad.

Because the chicken salad is served warm, it feels quite substantial and works as a main course. Some rice on the side would be make it even more so.

2½ cups thinly sliced red cabbage (about ⅓ medium head)
½ cup shredded carrots (about 1 large carrot)
⅓ cup thinly sliced (on the diagonal) scallions (about 4, white and green parts)
1 teaspoon plus 3 Tablespoons low-salt soy sauce
3½ teaspoons sugar
   Kosher salt
1 clove garlic
1 1-inch piece fresh ginger, peeled and sliced
¼ cup packed cilantro leaves, plus 1 Tablespoon chopped
3 Tablespoons creamy peanut butter
1 Tablespoon fresh lemon juice
2 Tablespoons peanut oil
1 pound thinly sliced chicken breast
⅓ cup sliced almonds or chopped peanuts, toasted in a dry skillet over medium heat

In a bowl, combine the cabbage, carrots, scallions, 1 teaspoon soy sauce, 1 teaspoon sugar, and a big pinch of salt. In a small food processor, chop the garlic and ginger. Add the ¼ cup cilantro and chop thoroughly. Add the peanut butter, 1 tablespoon hot water, the lemon juice, 1 tablespoon oil, 3 tablespoons soy sauce, and 2½ teaspoons sugar. Pulse until well combined, scraping the bowl as needed.

In a large skillet over medium-high heat, heat 1 tablespoon oil. Season the chicken pieces with salt and cook on one side until the edges are white (1 to 2 minutes); turn and cook until just firm, another 1 to 2 minutes. Transfer to a cutting board and let rest for 3 to 4 minutes. Slice the chicken into generous ¼-inch strips and put them in a large bowl. Squeeze the cabbage mixture well and add it to the chicken, pour in the dressing, and toss well. Garnish with the remaining cilantro and the toasted almonds or peanuts.

—SUSIE MIDDLETON

Tuscan Grilled Chicken & Pepper Salad (Pollo Forte)

SERVES 6

This strikingly beautiful salad works well as part of a lunch buffet.

- 5 boneless, skinless chicken breast halves
  Extra-virgin olive oil
  Salt and freshly ground black pepper
- 1 red bell pepper
- 1 yellow bell pepper
- ½ green bell pepper, cored, seeded, and very thinly sliced
- 1 poblano chile
- ½ to 1 jalapeño chile
- ½ small red onion, thinly sliced
- ¼ cup red-wine vinegar
- 1 Tablespoon balsamic vinegar1
- 2 cloves garlic, finely chopped
- ½ teaspoon crushed red pepper flakes
- 20 red cherry tomatoes, halved
- 20 yellow cherry tomatoes, halved
- ¾ cup niçoise, kalamata, or other good-quality black olives, pitted
- 30 basil leaves, washed, dried, and torn into small pieces

Core, seed, and thinly slice the bell peppers and chiles. Heat a gas or charcoal grill to medium hot. Lightly brush the chicken with olive oil. Grill the chicken breasts on one side for 4 to 5 minutes. Season with salt and pepper, then turn them over, and grill until cooked through, 3 to 4 minutes. Let cool and cut the chicken on the diagonal into thin slices. Put the chicken in a large bowl along with the bell peppers, chiles, and onion.

Whisk together the two vinegars, garlic, crushed red pepper flakes, and ¼ cup extra-virgin olive oil. Toss the vinaigrette with the chicken and peppers and let stand 30 minutes to an hour. Add the tomatoes, olives, and basil. Gently toss, season to taste with salt and pepper, and let stand another 15 minutes before serving.

—JOANNE WEIR

COOKING RIGHT

Grilling gives the chicken a caramelized crust that not only adds flavor, but also adds a pleasing texture. Boneless breasts cook and slice evenly.

COOKING AHEAD

You can't make a warm salad ahead of time. But you can make the dressing a couple hours ahead and keep it at room temperature.

Chicken-Mesclun Salad with Hazelnut Dressing

SERVES 4

COOK'S CHOICE

Use leftover roasted chicken pulled off of the bone in place of the sautéed breast.

You can find hazelnut oil at some supermarkets and specialty grocers; toasted hazelnut oil will give you the most flavor. But you can also use more olive oil in place of the nut oil.

For the dressing:
- 2 Tablespoons red-wine vinegar
- 2 cloves garlic, chopped
- 1 shallot, chopped
- 1 teaspoon Dijon-style mustard
- ⅓ cup extra-virgin olive oil
- 2 Tablespoons hazelnut oil (or just use more olive oil)
- 1 teaspoon chopped fresh thyme
- 2 teaspoons chopped fresh basil
  Salt and freshly ground black pepper

For the salad:
- ½ pound mesclun mix
- 3 Tablespoons olive oil
- 4 boneless, skinless chicken breasts (4 ounces each)
- 2 large portabella mushrooms, thinly sliced
- ½ red onion, thinly sliced
- ½ cup (1¾ ounces) grated aged Gouda
- ½ cup toasted chopped hazelnuts

HOW TO PLATE THIS SALAD

Use tongs. Tongs allow you to evenly distribute ingredients, including those that tend to fall to the bottom of the bowl.

Fan the chicken. It takes just a couple of seconds to arrange the chicken on the greens, yet it makes such a difference in how attractive the salad is.

Reserve some of the garnishes. Then you have some nice pieces to sprinkle over the assembled salad.

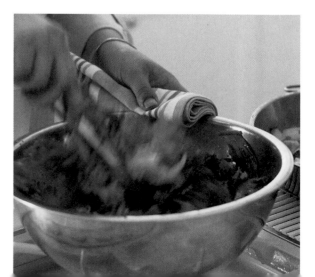

Make the dressing—In a medium bowl, whisk together the vinegar, garlic, shallot, and mustard. Slowly whisk in the oils until emulsified. Add the herbs, season with salt and pepper, and mix well. Set aside.

Make the salad—Put the mesclun in a large mixing bowl; set aside. In a large sauté pan, heat 2 tablespoons of the olive oil over high heat until very hot. Add the chicken and sear well, about 2 to 3 minutes per side. Reduce the heat to medium low and continue cooking until the chicken is done, 5 to 8 minutes, depending on thickness. Transfer the chicken to a cutting board, let rest 5 minutes, and slice thinly on the bias. Add the remaining 1 tablespoon oil to the sauté pan, turn the heat to medium high, and add the mushrooms and red onion. Sauté until tender, about 4 minutes. Reduce the heat to low, pour in the dressing, and heat just through. Pour the mushroom and onion mixture and about three-quarters of the liquid from the pan onto the greens and toss well to gently wilt them. Divide the salad among 4 serving plates. Top with the sliced chicken, cheese, and hazelnuts. Drizzle the remainder of the dressing over the chicken and serve immediately.

—CAPRIAL PENCE

COOK'S CHOICE

Try Gorgonzola in place of the Gouda, chanterelles in lieu of porta-bellas, or baby spinach instead of mesclun mix.

Updated Chef Salad

SERVES 4 TO 6

This chef's salad takes a fresh approach to an old standby.

¼ pound thinly sliced roasted turkey breast
¼ pound thinly sliced smoked ham
¼ pound thinly sliced dry sausage, such as spicy soppressata
10 cups lightly packed mixed greens, such as mesclun
2 cups cherry tomatoes, halved
6 ounces small mozzarella balls (bocconcini)
1 roasted red pepper, peeled, seeded, and thinly sliced
12 niçoise or other good-quality black olives, pitted
2 hard-cooked eggs, peeled and quartered lengthwise
   Croutons (optional)
   Kosher salt and freshly ground black pepper
1 cup Lemon Poppyseed Dressing (see recipe at left)
⅓ cup minced fresh herbs (such as a mix of parsley, mint, and chives)

Lemon Poppyseed Dressing

YIELDS ABOUT 1 CUP

Juice of 1 lemon (about ¼ cup)
2 Tablespoons heavy cream
1 teaspoon poppy seeds
1 teaspoon minced shallots
½ teaspoon finely grated lemon zest
¾ teaspoon kosher salt
   About 5 grinds of black pepper
¾ cup canola oil

Combine all but the oil together. Whisking constantly, add the oil in a slow, steady stream. Adjust seasonings to taste.

Stack the turkey slices and cut them into ¾-inch strips; repeat with the ham and the dry sausage. Toss to combine thoroughly. Put the salad greens in a large, shallow bowl. Arrange the tomatoes, mozzarella, roasted red pepper, olives, egg wedges, and croutons (if using) over the greens. Scatter the meats on top. Sprinkle the salad with salt and a few generous grinds of pepper. Drizzle with ½ cup of the dressing and sprinkle with the herbs. At the table, toss and serve the salad and pass with the remaining dressing.

—ABIGAIL JOHNSON DODGE

Sliced Salmon Salad with Olives & Tomatoes

SERVES 4

A quick poaching in a simple bouillon—salted water with bay leaf—accents the taste of the fish but does not alter its essential flavor.

For the fish:

1 salmon fillet (about 1 pound) cut in half lengthwise

1 quart water

2 Tablespoons kosher salt

2 bay leaves

For the tomato-olive garnish:

4 small ripe tomatoes (about ¾ pound total), peeled, seeded, and diced

½ cup pitted niçoise or other black olives

1 small shallot, minced

2 teaspoons red-wine vinegar or lemon juice

2 Tablespoons extra-virgin olive oil

Salt and freshly ground black pepper

1 Tablespoon chopped fresh parsley

For the watercress salad:

2 bunches fresh, tender watercress (about 10 ounces)

1 Tablespoon extra-virgin olive oil

1 teaspoon fresh lemon juice

COOKING RIGHT

Slice the salmon to the same thickness to ensure even cooking. Poaching pieces this size takes only about 2 minutes.

Slice the salmon on the bias ⅜-inch-thick. In a large skillet, bring the water, salt, and bay leaves to a boil over high heat. Add the fish and poach for 2 minutes. Remove with a slotted spatula to a plate lined with paper towels.

Combine the tomatoes, olives, shallot, vinegar, and olive oil. Season to taste with salt and pepper. Stir in the chopped parsley.

In a large pot of boiling water, wilt the watercress. Refresh it under cold water and pat dry. Toss with the olive oil and lemon juice and season to taste with more salt and pepper. On a platter or plates, arrange a bed of watercress, lay the salmon on top, and spoon the tomato-olive mixture over all.

—PAUL BERTOLLI

Crab & Avocado Salad

SERVES 4 AS A FIRST COURSE; 2 FOR LUNCH

Buy your avocado ahead to be sure it's ripe when you want it. To encourage ripening, put the avocado in a bag with a banana.

COOK'S CHOICE

For the best flavor, use fresh, non-pasteurized crabmeat. You can substitute thinly sliced shrimp or lobster for the crabmeat, if you like.

You can use heavy cream in place of the buttermilk; just add a few extra drops of lemon juice to mimic the buttermilk's tang.

3 Tablespoons mayonnaise
2 Tablespoons buttermilk
½ teaspoon grated lemon zest
2 teaspoons fresh lemon juice; more for sprinkling
½ teaspoon Dijon mustard
    Kosher salt and freshly ground black or white pepper
8 ounces crabmeat, preferably lump, picked over to remove bits of shell
½ cup finely chopped celery from the inner ribs and leaves
3 Tablespoons chopped fresh chives (½-inch pieces)
1 ripe avocado, peeled, pitted, and cut into ¾-inch pieces
1 head Boston or Bibb lettuce, washed (for lining the plates)

In a small bowl, whisk the mayonnaise, buttermilk, lemon zest, lemon juice, and mustard. Season with salt and pepper. In a medium bowl, mix the crabmeat, celery, and 2 tablespoons of the chives. Fold in the dressing gently so as not to break up the crabmeat. Gently fold in the avocado. Taste for salt and pepper. Line 4 salad plates with lettuce leaves, heap a scoop of the crab salad on each, and garnish with the remaining chives. Sprinkle each serving with ½ teaspoon lemon juice and serve.

—MOLLY STEVENS

Pasta Salad with Romesco Sauce & Roasted Red Peppers

SERVES 6

This spicy pasta is terrific on its own, but it's also a perfect foil for grilled shrimp. For steak or pork, grill the meat in one piece, slice it, and lay it over the pasta to let the juices blend in.

12 ounces dry orecchiette (little ear-shaped) pasta
6 Tablespoons extra-virgin olive oil
1 slice coarse-textured white bread
¼ cup skinned almonds
1 cup fresh or canned peeled, seeded, chopped, and drained tomatoes
1 clove garlic, minced
2 teaspoons sweet paprika
½ teaspoon crushed red pepper flakes
4 Tablespoons Spanish sherry vinegar
  Kosher salt and freshly ground black pepper
3 red bell peppers roasted as directed on p. 29 and cut into strips
¼ cup coarsely chopped flat-leaf parsley; more whole leaves for garnish

Bring a large pot of salted water to a boil. Add the orecchiette and cook until al dente, 10 to 12 minutes. Drain the pasta and toss immediately with 1 tablespoon of the olive oil. Refrigerate the pasta and cool it completely.

Heat 1 tablespoon of the olive oil in a small skillet over medium heat. Add the bread and fry, turning occasionally, until golden on both sides. Transfer the bread to a food processor. In the same skillet, fry the almonds, stirring until golden, about 2 minutes. Add the almonds, tomatoes, garlic, paprika, and red pepper flakes to the processor and pulse several times. In a small bowl, combine the vinegar with the remaining 4 tablespoons olive oil. With the processor running, gradually pour in the olive oil mixture until well combined and smooth. Season with salt and pepper. Let sit for 1 hour before using.

In a large bowl, toss together the orecchiette, peppers, sauce, and the chopped parsley. Season to taste with salt and pepper and garnish with the whole parsley leaves.

—JOANNE WEIR

COOKING RIGHT

Use a blender or a food processor to quickly and thoroughly purée the romesco sauce.

COOKING AHEAD

The various components *must* be made ahead, but they can sit longer (up to a day) than the minimum times suggested in the recipe.

COOKING RIGHT

To cut a chiffonade: Stack up to 10 basil leaves in a neat pile and roll them lengthwise into a tight cigar shape. Use your sharpest knife to slice across the cigar. The closer the slices the thinner the chiffonade.

Shrimp Bread Salad
with Golden Garlic Vinaigrette

SERVES 4

*Choose the ripest, fleshiest tomatoes you can find
so the bread soaks up their juices.*

1½ pounds large shrimp in the shell or about 42 frozen,
    cleaned large shrimp, defrosted
    About 5 thick slices day-old country-style bread,
    cut into ¾-inch cubes (about 7 cups)
3   large ripe tomatoes, cut into chunks
7   Tablespoons extra-virgin olive oil
4   teaspoons finely chopped garlic
½   teaspoon Spanish or Hungarian sweet paprika
2   Tablespoons aged sherry vinegar (or red-wine vinegar)
1   Tablespoon fresh lemon juice
    Salt and freshly ground black pepper
2   teaspoons fresh thyme leaves
1   cup loosely packed basil leaves, cut in a chiffonade

Heat the oven to 350°F. If using shrimp in the shell, peel and devein them (see the photos at the top of the facing page). If using cleaned, defrosted shrimp, skip this step. Either way, dry the shrimp well with paper towels and set aside.

Put the bread cubes on a baking sheet and toast them in the oven until they've dried out and turned golden brown, 14 to 18 minutes. Remove them from the oven. When cool, combine the bread with the tomatoes in a large bowl. Set aside.

Set a small, heavy skillet over low heat with 6 tablespoons of the olive oil and the chopped garlic. Cook, stirring or shaking the pan frequently, until the garlic turns a pale gold, 6 to 7 minutes. Bear in mind that the garlic will continue to cook from the retained heat of the pan. Remove the pan from the heat, stir in the paprika, vinegar, and lemon juice. Season well with salt and pepper. Pour half of the mixture (about ¼ cup) over the bread and tomatoes. Stir well to combine and set the remaining vinaigrette aside.

Set a large skillet over high heat with the remaining 1 tablespoon of olive oil. When the oil is hot, add the shrimp, season with salt and pepper, and sauté, stirring occasionally, until they're just cooked through and opaque, 3 to 4 minutes; cut one in half to check. Remove the pan from the heat. Add the remaining garlic vinaigrette to the pan, stir with the shrimp, taste, and adjust seasonings, if necessary.

Add the shrimp, thyme leaves, and basil to the bread and tomatoes. Toss and serve immediately.

—LESLIE REVSIN

PEELING AND DEVEINING SHRIMP

1 Start peeling underneath, where their legs are attached. Leave the last tail segment on for more flavor and good looks.

2 Devein by making a shallow slit down the middle of the back to expose the black intestine. (To butterfly, simply make this slit deeper.)

3 Lift out the black vein with the point of a paring knife and wipe if off on a paper towel, or rinse the vein out under cold running water.

SOUPS

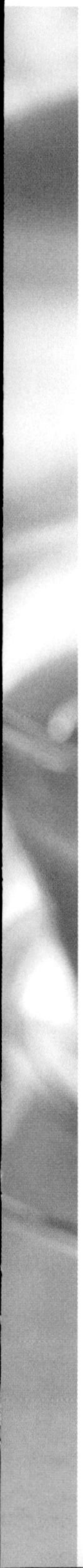

Chicken noodle soup, black bean soup, gazpacho, pasta e fagioli.
You'll find these familiar soups among the recipes in this chapter
but with a delicious twist that makes them feel fresh. Most of these
soups are very quick to prepare from start to finish with the help
of good-quality prepared products. So whether you are in the mood
to make a soup that needs a long slow simmer or one that comes
together in minutes for a satisfying weeknight meal, there's a soup
here for you.

THE RECIPES

Baked Potato & Leek Soup with Cheddar & Bacon

Quick "Manhattan" Clam Chowder

Chicken & Tortilla Soup

Chicken Noodle Soup with Ginger, Shiitakes & Leeks

Puréed Corn Soup with Roasted Red Pepper Coulis

Black Bean Soup with Tomato-Tomatillo Salsa

Escarole & White Bean "Soup" with Rustic Croutons

Yellow Tomato Gazpacho

Spicy Pasta e Fagioli

Garlicky Tortellini, Spinach & Tomato Soup

Baked Potato & Leek Soup with Cheddar & Bacon

YIELDS ABOUT 6 CUPS; SERVES 4

The whole potato, skin and all, goes into this thick soup, so wash the potatoes well.

2 medium russet potatoes (about ½ pound each)
4 Tablespoons unsalted butter
2 medium leeks (white and light green parts), sliced and rinsed well
2 medium cloves garlic, minced
   Kosher salt and freshly ground black pepper
2 cups homemade or low-salt canned chicken broth
4 thick slices bacon, cut into ½-inch dice
½ cup milk
½ cup sour cream
1 cup grated sharp Cheddar (about ¼ pound)
2 Tablespoons thinly sliced scallion greens or chives

Heat the oven to 375°F. Scrub the potatoes, pat dry, and pierce several times with a fork. Set them directly on the oven rack and bake until very tender, about 1 hour. Let cool completely on a cooling rack.

Melt the butter in a soup pot over medium-low heat. Add the leeks and garlic, season with salt, and cook, stirring occasionally, until softened, about 10 minutes. Add the broth and 2 cups water. Simmer until the leeks are very tender, about 20 minutes.

Meanwhile, cook the bacon over medium heat, stirring occasionally, until browned and crisp. Transfer to a paper-towel lined plate to drain.

Cut one of cooled potatoes in half lengthwise and scoop the flesh out in one piece from each half. Cut the flesh into ½-inch cubes and set aside. Coarsely chop the potato skin and the entire remaining potato and add to the pot with the leeks. Purée the contents of the pot in batches in a blender until very smooth. Return the soup to a clean pot and reheat over medium low. Whisk together the milk and sour cream and then whisk this into the soup, along with ½ cup of the Cheddar. Stir in the diced potato. Season with salt and pepper. Serve garnished with the remaining Cheddar, the bacon bits, and the scallions or chives.

—JENNIFER ARMENTROUT

COOK'S CHOICE

Sharp cheese works well in this soup because it melts smoothly. Extra sharp will give you a more pronounced flavor but because of its lower moisture content, the soup will be less smooth.

Be sure to cook the flour for the full minute to eliminate any raw flour taste. Stirring constantly will keep it from burning. (A straight-edged wooden spoon is great for this task.)

Quick "Manhattan" Clam Chowder

SERVES 4

Using canned clams allows you to make this robust, colorful soup in a matter of minutes.

2 ounces bacon, cut into ½-inch pieces

1 medium onion, diced

½ large red bell pepper, diced

3 Tablespoons all-purpose flour

4 cans (6½ ounces each) minced clams, clams and juice separated (about 1½ cups minced clams and 2¼ cups juice)

1 bottle (8 ounces) clam juice

1 can (14½ ounces) diced tomatoes, with their liquid

3 small boiling potatoes (about ¾ pound), cut into a medium dice

¼ teaspoon dried thyme

2 Tablespoons minced fresh flat-leaf parsley
    Coarse salt and freshly ground black pepper

In a Dutch oven or a large saucepan, fry the bacon over medium heat until the fat renders and the bacon crisps, about 7 minutes. With a slotted spoon, transfer the bacon to a small bowl; set aside.

Add the onion and bell pepper to the bacon drippings; sauté until softened, about 5 minutes. Add the flour and stir until lightly colored, about 1 minute. Gradually whisk in the clam juice (from the cans and the bottle) and ½ cup water and then add the tomatoes, potatoes, and thyme.

Simmer until the potatoes are tender, about 10 minutes. Add the clams and parsley, season with salt and pepper; and bring to a simmer. Remove the pot from the heat, ladle the chowder into bowls, sprinkle with the reserved bacon, and serve.

—PAM ANDERSON

Chicken & Tortilla Soup

SERVES 2 AS A LIGHT MAIN COURSE OR SUBSTANTIAL FIRST COURSE

Be sure the broth is very hot so that it heats up the ingredients in the bowl and offers a strong contrast with the cool, smooth chunks of avocado. This recipe is easily doubled.

- 1 Tablespoon vegetable or olive oil, plus another ½ to 1 cup for frying the tortillas
- ¼ cup finely chopped onion
- 1 Tablespoon chile powder; more to taste
- 1 Tablespoon tomato paste
- 2 skinless chicken thighs (bone-in or boneless)
  Salt
- 4 cups homemade or low-salt canned chicken broth
  Fresh cilantro: six 2-inch stems for the broth, plus ¼ cup roughly chopped leaves for the garnish
- 4 fresh corn tortillas, 6 inches across, cut into ¼-inch-wide strips
- ½ cup corn kernels (fresh, frozen, or canned)
- ½ cup canned black beans, rinsed and drained
- ¾ cup diced fresh tomato

For the garnish:

- 1 ripe avocado, diced and tossed with a squeeze of lime juice
- ¼ cup crumbled queso fresco, feta, or ricotta salata
- 2 dollops sour cream
  Lime wedges for serving

HOW TO CRISP TORTILLA

Heat about an inch of oil in a high-sided saucepan over medium heat. When a tortilla sizzles immediately on contact with the oil, add six to eight strips to the pan. With tongs or a long fork, "scrunch" them for a second or so to make them wavy as in the top left photo. Fry until the strips are no longer bubbling much and have become light brown. Drain on paper towels and continue with the rest of the strips.

Put 1 tablespoon of the oil in a large saucepan or small soup pot, add the onion, and cook over medium heat until the onion has softened but not browned, about 3 minutes. Add the chile powder and tomato paste and stir with a wooden spoon to mix and cook briefly; take care not to let the chile powder scorch.

Season the chicken thighs lightly with salt and nestle them in the chile paste, turning them once so they're entirely coated. Pour in about ½ cup of the broth and adjust the heat to a simmer. Cover the pan and cook the chicken, turning once, until it's extremely tender when pierced with a knife, 30 to 40 minutes (add a little more broth if the pan is drying out). When the chicken is done, remove it from the pan, let it cool a bit, and cut or shred it into bite-size pieces, discarding any bones and bits of fat or gristle; set aside.

Spoon off any visible grease in the pan, add the remaining broth and the cilantro stems, and simmer, uncovered, until the broth has reduced by about one-third and is quite flavorful, 20 to 30 minutes.

While the broth is reducing, fry the tortillas (see the sidebar on the facing page).

Divide the shredded chicken, the corn, black beans, tomato, and tortilla strips between two large soup or pasta bowls. Reheat the broth if necessary so it's piping hot and pour it over the ingredients in the bowls. Serve immediately, and let each diner add the avocado, cheese, sour cream, chopped cilantro, and a big squeeze of lime juice at the table.

—MARTHA HOLMBERG

COOK'S CHOICE

Try rib-eye (about 8 ounces) in place of the chicken. Cut it into bite-size strips, toss it with a little salt, and sauté it briefly in a little oil as the initial step. Remove the meat and continue with the recipe—skipping the chicken, of course.

Chicken Noodle Soup with Ginger, Shiitakes & Leeks

SERVES 4 TO 6

Layers of sweet, sour, salty, and spicy ingredients make a full flavored broth that comes together surprisingly quickly.

¾ ounce dried shiitake mushrooms (about 12)

5 bone-in chicken thighs (1½ to 2 pounds) skin removed, fat trimmed
   Kosher salt and freshly ground black pepper

2 teaspoons peanut or vegetable oil

1 large or 2 small leeks (white and light green parts only), sliced into thin half moons and washed

3 Tablespoons minced fresh ginger

4 cups homemade or low-salt canned chicken broth

¼ cup mirin or rice wine

2 Tablespoons soy sauce

1 Tablespoon rice vinegar

1 teaspoon Asian chile paste

9 ounces fresh Chinese egg noodles, other Asian noodle, or linguine or spaghetti

1 teaspoon toasted sesame oil

2 scallions, thinly sliced on the bias (about ⅓ cup)

Put the shiitakes in a bowl and cover with about 1½ cups boiling water. Set a small plate or pot lid over the mushrooms to ensure they're submerged, and soak until softened, about 20 minutes. Discard the mushroom stems and thinly slice the caps. Strain the soaking liquid through a fine mesh strainer, leaving any sediment behind. Reserve the liquid and shiitakes separately.

Rinse the chicken thighs and pat dry with paper towels; season with salt. Heat the oil in a heavy soup pot or Dutch oven over medium-low heat. When the oil is hot, add the chicken, cover the pot, and cook for about 10 minutes, turning once or twice. The aim is to sweat (not brown) the

chicken until it loses its raw pink color on the outside and begins to exude some of its juices. Stir in the leeks, ginger, and sliced shiitakes; cover and cook until the leeks begin to soften, about another 5 minutes.

Add the broth, 3 cups of water, reserved mushroom soaking liquid, mirin, soy sauce, vinegar, and chile paste, and bring to a gentle boil over high heat. Adjust the heat to maintain a gentle simmer and cook uncovered until the chicken is very tender and falling off the bone, about 45 minutes. Remove the chicken and set it aside.

Meanwhile, bring a large pot of well-salted water to a boil. Cook the egg noodles until just tender, about 3 minutes. (Cook other noodles according to the package directions.) Drain and rinse under cold water.

When the chicken is cool enough to handle, remove the meat from the bones and roughly chop or tear it into bite-size pieces. Return the meat to the soup. Add the sesame oil and season the soup with salt and pepper.

Stir the noodles into the soup and let them heat through. Ladle the soup into bowls, top with the sliced scallions, and serve immediately.

—EVA KATZ

COOKING RIGHT

Don't be tempted to cook the noodles right in the soup or the soup will become too starchy. Add cooked noodles just before serving.

ASIAN CHILE PASTES PACK A PUNCH

What are they? Primarily puréed chiles with oil or vinegar and salt. They may also contain sugar, garlic, ginger, or soybeans. Be sure the first ingredient is chiles.

Where do I get them? At Asian markets and some supermarkets.

How hot are they? Very. Use the amount suggested (or even a bit less) until you can gauge how you like the heat.

How long do they keep? Indefinitely if refrigerated and tightly covered.

Puréed Corn Soup with Roasted Red Pepper Coulis

SERVES 4; YIELDS ½ CUP COULIS

This is a perfect soup for late summer.

For the coulis:

  1 small clove garlic
  ½ teaspoon kosher salt
  1 small roasted red pepper (see p. 29)
1½ teaspoons balsamic vinegar
  ¼ teaspoon red-wine vinegar
  ⅛ teaspoon freshly ground black pepper
     Pinch cayenne
  1 teaspoon extra-virgin olive oil

For the soup:

  3 ears corn (2¼ cups kernels)
  8 sprigs fresh basil; more tiny leaves for garnish
10 sprigs fresh thyme
  1 bay leaf
  3 Tablespoons unsalted butter
  1 medium onion, sliced (1 cup)
     Kosher salt
  1 Tablespoon minced fresh garlic

Make the red pepper coulis—Mash the garlic with ¼ teaspoon salt to a fine paste in a mortar and pestle or with the side of a chef's knife. Put the garlic paste, the red pepper, ¼ teaspoon salt, the balsamic vinegar, red-wine vinegar, black pepper, cayenne, and olive oil in a blender. Blend on high speed to a smooth purée.

Make the soup—Shuck the corn and rub off the silk. Stand one ear on a board or in a shallow bowl and with a knife, slice straight down the ear to remove the kernels. Turn the ear and repeat until all the kernels are removed. Scrape the dull side of the knife down the cob to extract the corn "milk."

COOKING AHEAD

A puréed vegetable soup will hold up well for a couple of days in the refrigerator, but it might separate. Simply use a whisk or an immersion blender to emulsify it before serving.

Don't bother picking the prettiest pepper since it will be roasted and puréed.

Put the cobs (broken in half, if necessary), the herbs, and 5 cups water in a large saucepan or a stockpot. Bring to a boil, reduce to a simmer, and cook uncovered for 15 minutes. Remove the cobs and strain the broth.

Melt the butter in a large, heavy saucepan set over medium heat. Add the onion and 2 teaspoons salt, cover, and cook, stirring occasionally, until the onion is translucent, about 5 minutes; don't let it brown. Stir in the garlic and 2¼ cups corn kernels with the "milk." Add enough of the herb broth to cover the corn, bring to a simmer, and cook until the corn is very tender, 17 to 20 minutes.

Purée the corn in batches in a blender and strain it thorough a fine mesh strainer, pressing down on the soup with a rubber spatula.

Taste the soup and add salt, if necessary. Serve warm, garnished with a swirl of the red pepper coulis and several tiny basil leaves.

—EVE FELDER

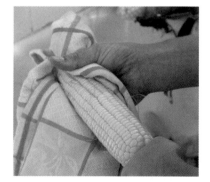

TIPS TO GET CORN OFF THE COB

To keep your kernels from flying around the kitchen as you cut, follow these tips.

- Keep the stem on to use as a handle.

- Rub the ear briskly with a dry towel to remove any stubborn silks.

- Rest the ear firmly in a bowl (a damp towel under the bowl keeps it from slipping) and cut from stem to tip. Don't cut the cob or you'll include tough woody bits.

- Use the dull side of the knife to scrape the cob and extract the corn "milk."

Black Bean Soup with Tomato-Tomatillo Salsa

YIELDS ABOUT 6 CUPS

COOKING RIGHT

Soaking makes a difference.
Soak the beans for at least 8 hours.
A soak speeds up cooking and
makes the beans much more tender.

A vibrant garnish literally brightens up this soup and adds a nice crisp contrast to the softer texture of the beans.

1   pound dried black beans
2   Tablespoons vegetable oil
2   large onions, finely diced
4   to 6 cloves garlic, minced
1   cup peeled, seeded, and chopped tomato, fresh or canned
    Small sprig fresh or dried epazote (optional)
1   Tablespoon finely chopped canned chipotle chile (or ¼ teaspoon cayenne)
1   teaspoon ground cumin seed
1   teaspoon ground coriander
2   teaspoons salt

For the salsa:
1   large tomato, finely diced
3   medium tomatillos, husks removed and finely diced
1   small red onion, very finely diced
1   serrano or jalapeño chile, very finely diced
¼   cup roughly chopped fresh cilantro leaves
    Salt

For the garnish:
    Crème fraîche or sour cream

To make the soup—Soak the beans for at least 8 and up to 24 hours, and drain.

In a deep, heavy-based pot, heat the oil over medium heat. Add the onions and cook until translucent, about 5 minutes. Add the beans, garlic, and 6 cups cold water. Bring to a boil, skimming any foam that rises to

the surface. Reduce to a simmer and when the beans are soft, after about 1 hour, add the tomato, epazote (if using), chipotle chile, cumin, coriander, and salt. Continue cooking until the beans start to break down and the broth begins to thicken. Taste for seasoning; add salt and pepper if needed. If you're serving this soup immediately, you may want to thicken it by puréeing a cup or two of the beans in a blender or food processor and then recombine with the rest of the soup. The soup will thicken on its own if refrigerated overnight.

To make the salsa—In a small bowl, combine the tomato, tomatillos, onion, jalapeño, and cilantro. Taste for seasoning and add salt as needed. This salsa will taste best if assembled no more than an hour before serving.

Ladle the soup into individual serving bowls and garnish each portion with a spoonful of crème fraîche and the salsa.

—DAVID TANIS

AUTHENTIC MEXICAN INGREDIENTS

Epazote, an herb often used in Mexican cooking, adds an authentic, musky undertone to the soup, but the soup is delicious without it.

Canned chiptole chiles add a distinctively smoky flavor, but using a little cayenne pepper in its place will still give you a spicy kick.

You can find tomatillos, also called Mexican green tomatos, in the produce section of most supermarkets. If you can't find them, add another tomato to the salsa.

Escarole & White Bean "Soup" with Rustic Croutons

SERVES 4

Rustic Croutons

2 Tablespoons extra-virgin olive oil
2 cups ¾-inch cubes of bread
   cut from a country-style loaf
   Salt

Heat oil in a nonstick skillet over medium-high heat. Add the bread cubes. Stir to coat with the oil, season with salt, and cook until browned.

This is a variation on a classic Italian soup that traditionally has more escarole and beans than broth.

¼ cup extra-virgin olive oil
1 medium onion, diced
2 ounces very thinly sliced pancetta, diced (about 1/2 cup)
1 Tablespoon minced garlic
1 medium head escarole (about 14 ounces), trimmed, leaves sliced
   across into ¾-inch-wide strips and very thoroughly washed
1 teaspoon coarse salt
   Freshly ground black pepper
2 cups low-salt chicken stock
1 cup cooked or canned small white beans
1 Tablespoon fresh lemon juice
¼ cup grated Parmigiano Reggiano
2 cups Rustic Croutons (see recipe at left)

Heat the olive oil in a 4-quart, low-sided soup pot or Dutch oven over medium heat. Add the onion and pancetta and sauté until the onion is softened and both are browned, about 12 minutes. Add the garlic, stir, and sauté until fragrant, 30 seconds to 1 minute. Add the escarole and stir thoroughly to coat the leaves. Season with ½ teaspoon of the salt and a few grinds of fresh pepper. Add the stock, stir well, and bring to a boil; cover the pot, lower to a simmer, and cook 8 to 10 minutes. Uncover the pot, add the beans, and simmer another 2 to 3 minutes. Add the lemon juice and turn off the heat. Ladle the soup into four shallow soup bowls and top each with 1 tablespoon of the cheese and a quarter of the croutons.

—SUSIE MIDDLETON

Yellow Tomato Gazpacho

YIELDS ABOUT 9 CUPS

Sometimes called a "liquid salad," gazpacho is one of the most refreshing soups.

3½ pound ripe yellow tomatoes, peeled, seeded, and chopped
1 yellow bell pepper, cored, seeded, and coarsely chopped
1 red onion, coarsely chopped
1 cucumber, peeled, seeded, and chopped
¼ cup white-wine vinegar
3 large cloves garlic, finely chopped
3 Tablespoons extra-virgin olive oil
1 slice stale bread (crust removed), soaked in water and squeezed dry
   Salt and freshly ground black pepper

For the garnish:
1 Tablespoon unsalted butter
1 Tablespoon extra-virgin olive oil
3 cloves garlic, crushed
6 slices sourdough bread (crusts removed), torn into ¾-inch pieces
¼ cup diced green bell pepper
¼ cup peeled, seeded, and chopped cucumber
1½ cups cherry tomatoes, quartered (use a mix of colors)
¼ cup diced red onion

In a bowl, mix the tomatoes, yellow pepper, onion, cucumber, vinegar, garlic, olive oil, and bread. In a blender, purée the mixture in batches until very smooth. Pass through a coarse strainer. Stir in 2½ teaspoons salt and ½ teaspoon pepper. Refrigerate until well chilled.

Heat the oven to 375°F. In a small saucepan, heat the butter and oil over medium-high heat. Add the garlic and cook, stirring, about 1 minute. Discard the garlic. Spread the bread pieces on a baking sheet, drizzle with the butter, and toss well. Bake, tossing occasionally, until golden, 10 to 12 minutes. Ladle the chilled soup into bowls and garnish with the toasted bread, green pepper, cucumber, tomatoes, and red onion.

—JOANNE WEIR

COOKING AHEAD

The soup has to be made at least a little while ahead so that it can be chilled, but it will keep a couple of days in the fridge. Taste the soup before serving as cold can mute flavor; add more salt, pepper, or vinegar if needed.

COOKING RIGHT

Blanching tomatoes (a quick boil followed by an ice bath plunge) makes them much easier to peel.

COOK'S CHOICE

Any small-shape pasta would work
well in this soup, including ditalini,
tubettini, or even elbow macaroni.

Spicy Pasta e Fagioli

YIELDS 9 CUPS; SERVES 4

*Anchovies give this soup a full (but not fishy) flavor. If using salt-packed anchovies,
soak them in a few changes of water before using them to get rid of excess salt.*

¼ cup extra-virgin olive oil
2 cloves garlic, minced
1 to 1½ teaspoons freshly ground black pepper
¼ teaspoon dried red pepper flakes
½ cup finely chopped onion
1 2-ounce can anchovies, drained and chopped fine or mashed
2 15-ounce cans Great Northern or other white beans,
    with their liquid
¼ pound ditalini or other small pasta (about 1 cup dry), cooked
3 cups vegetable stock, chicken stock, or water
1 Tablespoon lemon juice
¼ cup chopped fresh parsley leaves
½ cup (about 2 ounces) grated Parmesan,
    preferably Parmigiano Reggiano
    Salt

In a large pot, heat the olive oil over medium-high heat. Sauté the garlic,
black pepper, and red pepper flakes for 30 seconds. Add the onion and
anchovies and sauté until the onion is soft and translucent, about 2 minutes.

Add the beans with their liquid, the ditalini, and
the stock. Let the mixture come to a boil, reduce
the heat, and simmer for 5 to 10 minutes. Just
before serving, stir in the lemon juice, parsley, and
¼ cup Parmesan. Taste, and add salt as necessary.
Serve hot, passing the remaining Parmesan at
the table.

—ROSINA TINARI WILSON

Garlicky Tortellini, Spinach & Tomato Soup

SERVES 2 TO 3

Make this practically instant soup the moment you feel a cold coming on. It tastes soothing and delicious, and the healthful properties of chicken broth, garlic, and spinach are bound to make you feel better faster.

2   Tablespoons unsalted butter
6   to 8 cloves garlic, chopped
4   cups homemade or low-salt chicken broth
6   ounces fresh or frozen cheese tortellini
14 ounces canned diced tomatoes, with their liquid
10 ounces spinach, washed and stemmed;
     coarsely chopped if large
8   to 10 leaves basil, coarsely chopped
     Grated Parmesan, preferably Parmigiano Reggiano

Melt the butter in a large saucepan over medium-high heat. Add the garlic and sauté until fragrant, about 2 minutes. Add the broth and bring to a boil. Add the tortellini and cook halfway, about 5 minutes for frozen pasta, less if using fresh. Add the tomatoes and their liquid, reduce the heat to a simmer, and cook just until the pasta is tender. Stir in the spinach and basil and cook until wilted, 1 to 2 minutes. Serve sprinkled with the grated cheese.

—JOANNE SMART

COOKING RIGHT

Get rid of tough stems. If using older (not baby) spinach, remove the stem completely by folding the leaf in half lengthwise, pulling on the stalk like a zipper moving down the leaf.

PASTA

Although we can thank Italy for pasta, polenta, and risotto, American cooks have embraced these classic comfort foods, making them their own in such recipes as squash-stuffed ravioli with walnuts and cranberries, orzo teamed with shiitakes, spinach and Asian flavorings, and a gorgonzola "mac and cheese." There are suggestions in the pasta recipes about when to cook the pasta, but you can change the order to fit your schedule. Your best bet is to read through each recipe and decide for yourself how to proceed.

THE RECIPES

Orzo with Spinach, Shiitakes & Caramelized Onions

Linguine with Asparagus, Morels & Cream

Angel Hair Pasta with Mussels & Spicy Tomato Sauce

Penne with Grilled Vegetables & Garlic-Rubbed Bread

Fusilli with Feta & Lemon-Caper Pesto

Squash Ravioli with Sherried Onion Sauce, Walnuts & Cranberries

Shells with Gorgonzola

Pappardelle with Shrimp & Zucchini

Linguine with Leeks, Prosciutto & Lemon

Cavatelli with Arugula & Ricotta Salata

Gratin of Polenta with Greens

Creamy Goat Cheese Polenta

Wild Mushroom Risotto

Risotto of Sweet Sausage & Broccoli Raab

Risotto with Corn, Tomatoes & Basil

Orzo with Spinach, Shiitakes & Caramelized Onions

SERVES 8 AS A SIDE DISH

*Orzo, a little rice-shaped pasta, pairs wonderfully well with Asian flavors.
Try this as a delicious, colorful side dish to a seared or grilled steak.*

COOKING RIGHT

Smell your sesame seeds for
freshness before adding them to
any dish. They can keep for months
stored in a dark, cool place, but as
they are half oil, they can become
rancid.

Toast sesame seeds in a dry skillet
over low heat or in a 350°F oven,
stirring occasionally. But keep your
eye on them: They burn easily.

Be sure to use toasted sesame oil—
it will look quite dark—for the best
flavor.

Kosher salt
3 Tablespoons soy sauce
1 Tablespoon rice vinegar
1 teaspoon toasted sesame oil
5 Tablespoons peanut oil
2 cloves garlic, smashed
1 Tablespoon grated fresh ginger
Pinch crushed red chile flakes
6 ounces fresh shiitake mushrooms, stemmed, cleaned, and thinly sliced
2 Tablespoons dry sherry (or dry white wine)
Freshly ground black pepper
1 large yellow onion, finely diced
10 ounces spinach, stemmed, washed, and coarsely chopped
1 pound dried orzo
2 scallions (white and green parts), thinly sliced
1 teaspoon toasted sesame seeds (optional)
1 lime, cut into small wedges

Bring a large pot of well-salted water to a boil. In a small bowl, whisk
together the soy sauce, rice vinegar, sesame oil, and 2 tablespoons of the
peanut oil.

Set a large skillet or wok over medium-high heat. When the pan is hot,
pour in 1½ tablespoons of the peanut oil and, after a few seconds, add
the garlic, ginger, and chile flakes. Stir for 20 seconds, making sure that
the garlic doesn't burn. Add the mushrooms and stir-fry until they soften,
2 to 3 minutes. Add the sherry and cook for another 30 seconds. Season

with salt and pepper and transfer the mixture to a bowl. Reduce the heat to medium, heat the remaining 1½ tablespoons oil in the pan, and add the onions. Season with salt and then sauté them, stirring often, until they're soft and slightly caramelized, 9 to 10 minutes. Add the spinach, cover the pan, and steam, shaking the pan occasionally, until the spinach wilts, about 3 minutes. Remove and discard the garlic from the mushrooms, put the mushrooms back in the pan, and toss. Remove from the heat and season lightly with salt and pepper. Reserve until needed.

Cook the orzo in the boiling water until it's just tender, about 9 minutes. Drain it well and put it in a large bowl. Add the mushroom mixture, soy vinaigrette, scallions, and sesame seeds (if using) and toss. Taste and season. Serve with lime wedges to squeeze over the pasta.

—TONY ROSENFELD

COOKING AHEAD

This dish has such an abundance of flavors that it tastes great at practically any temperature, making it quite flexible: Serve it hot, warm, or even at room temperature.

COOKING RIGHT

Asparagus keeps longer if its stem ends are submerged, flower-like, in water.

Linguine with Asparagus, Morels & Cream

SERVES 2

If you can't find fresh morels, use dried. Chanterelles also taste great in this dish.

3 ounces fresh morel mushrooms, wiped clean, or 1 ounce dried morels, reconstituted in 2 cups of hot water, drained (strain and reserve the liquid), and patted dry

4 Tablespoons unsalted butter

1 small shallot, finely chopped (about 1 Tablespoon)

1 pound asparagus, trimmed and cut on the diagonal into 1½-inch slices

1¼ cups heavy cream

2 teaspoons fresh thyme leaves

Salt and freshly ground black pepper

6 ounces linguine or fettuccine

3 Tablespoons freshly grated Parmigiano Reggiano

If the morels are large, cut them in half lengthwise. Melt the butter in a large skillet over medium heat. Add the shallot and cook for about 1 minute. Add the morels and cook, stirring occasionally, until just tender, about 10 minutes. (If using dried morels, boil the strained soaking liquid until reduced to ¼ cup. Strain the liquid through a coffee filter and add it with the asparagus and cream for even more flavor.) Add the asparagus, cream, and thyme and simmer until the asparagus is just tender and the sauce is slightly thickened, about 5 minutes. Season generously with salt and pepper.

Meanwhile, cook the pasta until al dente, drain it, and toss it with the asparagus and morels. Add the cheese and toss to coat the pasta. Serve immediately in warm bowls.

—SEEN LIPPERT

Angel Hair Pasta with Mussels & Spicy Tomato Sauce

SERVES 4 AS A MAIN COURSE

Steaming the mussels directly in the pasta sauce streamlines the recipe and adds flavor.

2   Tablespoons olive oil

1   medium onion, chopped

1   small bulb fennel, chopped

2   Tablespoons anise-flavored liqueur, such as
    Pernod or ¼ teaspoon crushed fennel seeds

5   threads saffron, crushed and soaked in
    1 Tablespoon warm water

4   cloves garlic, minced

1   teaspoon chopped fresh thyme, or ¼ teaspoon dried

¾   cup crisp, dry white wine

1   28-ounce can whole plum tomatoes with liquid

1½ pounds medium mussels, cleaned and sorted

¾   pound angel hair pasta
    Salt and freshly ground black pepper

½   cup chopped parsley

Heat the olive oil in a large, deep skillet (with a lid) or a Dutch oven over medium heat. Add the onion and cook for 2 to 3 minutes. Add the fennel and cook until the onion is translucent, another 8 to 10 minutes. Increase the heat to high, add the Pernod, saffron, garlic, and thyme. After 1 minute, stir in the white wine and boil for 5 minutes. Add the tomatoes, reduce the heat, and simmer 15 to 20 minutes, stirring to break up the tomatoes.

Meanwhile, bring a large pot of well salted water to a boil. Scatter the mussels over the tomato sauce and cover the pot. Steam until the shells are open, 8 to 10 minutes. Season the sauce with salt and pepper and keep it warm while you cook the pasta until al dente. Divide the pasta and sauce among four serving bowls and sprinkle with chopped parsley. Serve immediately.

—MOLLY STEVENS

COOKING RIGHT

For a grit-free dish, scrub mussels well with a brush and snip off any tough beards before cooking.

COOKING RIGHT

Be sure to include the juices that accumulate as you chop the vegetables—especially the tomatoes—as they help to impart a wonderful smoky flavor.

Penne with Grilled Vegetables & Garlic-Rubbed Bread

SERVES 6

Two things make this pasta a stand-out: the unexpected sweet and smoky flavor of grilled fennel and the garlicky crunch of the grilled bread.

1   pound penne pasta
½   cup olive oil, more as needed
4   red bell peppers, cored, seeded, and quartered
1   head fennel, cut into 6 or 8 wedges
1   pound small zucchini, halved lengthwise
6   Roma or 3 larger tomatoes, cored
6   large scallions, trimmed to leave 3 inches green
     Salt and freshly ground black pepper
6   slices crusty Italian bread, 1 inch thick
2   cloves garlic, halved
1   medium bunch fresh basil, leaves washed, dried, and sliced
     Juice of ½ lemon
⅓   cup freshly grated Parmesan or ricotta salata

Bring a large pot of salted water to a boil. Cook the pasta until al dente. Drain it, put it in a large bowl, and drizzle it lightly with a little of the olive oil to prevent sticking.

Lightly oil the vegetables and season with salt and pepper. Grill all of the vegetables, turning occasionally, until soft and slightly charred; their times will vary. Chop the vegetables into chunks, and add them and any accumulated juices to the bowl with the pasta. Keep warm.

Meanwhile, lightly brush the bread with more olive oil and grill it on both sides. Rub with the cut garlic cloves.

Add the basil to the pasta and vegetables and toss to mix. Squeeze in some lemon juice, drizzle on a few more tablespoons of olive oil, and season with salt and pepper. Toss again and serve with the grilled garlic bread and grated cheese on the side.

—MOLLY STEVENS

Fusilli with Feta & Lemon-Caper Pesto

SERVES 4 AS A LIGHT MAIN COURSE

You can make the tangy, lemony pasta sauce in the time it takes to cook the pasta.

For the pasta:

Salt

½ pound dried fusilli pasta

1 bunch fresh spinach (10 ounces), stems cut off, leaves washed well but not dried

¼ pound feta, crumbled (⅔ cup)

For the pesto:

1 small clove garlic

2 to 3 anchovy fillets, rinsed and patted dry

1 Tablespoon capers, soaked briefly and rinsed

1 1-inch strip lemon zest, minced

¾ ounces feta, crumbled (2 Tablespoons)

¼ cup roughly chopped fresh flat-leaf parsley

2 or 3 fresh basil leaves (optional)

1 Tablespoon fresh lemon juice

¼ cup extra-virgin olive oil

Salt and freshly ground black pepper

Bring a pot of salted water to a boil and cook the pasta until al dente. Reserve ½ cup of the cooking water before draining the pasta, and don't wash the pot. Meanwhile, put the wet spinach in a large skillet over medium heat. Add a dash of salt, cover, and cook for 3 to 4 minutes. Remove the pan from the heat, but keep the lid on.

Put the garlic, anchovies, capers, lemon zest, 2 tablespoons feta, parsley, basil, lemon juice, olive oil, salt, and pepper in a blender and blend until the pesto is creamy. Thin the pesto with a little of the reserved pasta water to get the consistency of runny cream.

Return the pasta to its pot; add the spinach and the pesto, stirring very well to coat the pasta. Stir in the ⅔ cup crumbled feta and serve.

—DAPHNE ZEPOS

COOKING RIGHT

Thin the pesto with a little of the reserved pasta water; you probably won't need to use all of the water.

Squash Ravioli with Sherried Onion Sauce, Walnuts & Cranberries

YIELDS ABOUT 40 RAVIOLI

Wonton wrappers (or "pasta wraps"), found in the grocery produce section, give excellent results and are quick and easy to work with.

For the filling:
1 large or 2 small butternut squash (2½ pounds total), cut in half and seeded
5 to 6 Tablespoons unsalted butter, softened
⅓ cup maple syrup or 2 Tablespoons brown sugar
¼ cup orange juice
¼ cup ricotta
⅓ cup grated Parmesan
Salt and freshly ground black pepper

To assemble the ravioli:
Cornmeal for dusting
80 wonton wrappers ("pasta wraps")
2 eggs mixed with a dash of water

For the sauce:
2 large onions (14 to 16 ounces total), thinly sliced
3 Tablespoons unsalted butter; more if needed
⅓ cup dry sherry
1½ cups heavy cream
1½ cups homemade or low-salt canned chicken or vegetable stock
2 Tablespoons finely chopped fresh sage

For the garnish:
½ cup finely chopped toasted walnuts
½ cup finely chopped dried cranberries
2 Tablespoons chopped fresh chives
3 ounces Parmesan, shaved with a vegetable peeler into shards

TO ROAST SQUASH

Put seeded squash halves on a rimmed baking sheet. Rub the flesh with butter, maple syrup, and orange juice and then flip the halves over. Bake at 400°F until tender, about 45 minutes. Let cool a bit and peel off the charred skin.

COOKING AHEAD

The filling and the sauce can both be made a day ahead and refrigerated. (Reheat the sauce gently over low heat.) You can also freeze the filled, uncooked pasta for up to a month.

To make the filling—Follow the method for roasting squash on the facing page using the amounts for the squash, butter, maple syrup, and orange juice listed for the filling. Put the flesh and any juices from roasting into a large heavy-based sauté pan and cook over medium heat, stirring frequently and mashing the squash to dry out the mixture, about 10 minutes. Let cool. When cooled, mix in the two cheeses and season with salt and pepper.

To assemble the ravioli—Lightly dust your work surface and a sheet pan with cornmeal. Lay out 10 wrappers and brush five of them with egg wash. Place 1 scant tablespoon of the filling in the center of each piece of egg-washed pasta and flatten slightly. Quickly and gently cover each with a dry wrapper and press tightly around each mound and out toward the edges of the pasta to create a tight seal. If you like, trim the ravioli with a cookie cutter or knife. Arrange the filled ravioli in a single layer on the sheet pan. Cover and refrigerate or freeze until ready to use.

To make the sauce—Sauté the onions in 3 tablespoons of the butter over medium heat until very soft, 20 to 25 minutes. Add the sherry, raise the heat to medium high, and cook until all the liquid is evaporated. Add the cream and stock and the chopped sage, and cook until reduced by half. Season with salt and pepper and reserve.

To cook and serve the ravioli—Gently warm the sauce and have the garnishes ready. Bring a large pot of salted water to a boil, add a touch of olive oil, and drop in 4 to 6 ravioli at a time. When they rise to the surface, boil for 4 minutes and then remove them with a slotted spoon and transfer them to a strainer. Arrange 3 or 4 ravioli on a large plate for an appetizer (6 for a dinner portion), cover lightly with the sauce, and sprinkle with the walnuts, cranberries, and chives. Add a few shards of Parmesan and serve.

—RIS LACOSTE

COOKING RIGHT

To avoid air pockets, seal the ravioli by pressing down close to the filling first and then work your way out to seal the edges.

Slow and gentle heat makes a smooth cheese sauce.

Tangy blue cheese and toasted nuts give the topping crunch and zing.

Shells with Gorgonzola

SERVES 4 AS A SIDE DISH

This is wonderful as a side dish to a beef filet, but if you want to serve it as a main course, you can easily double the recipe.

8   ounces medium pasta shells
½   cup heavy cream
1   Tablespoon dry sherry (optional)
6   ounces Gorgonzola, crumbled
     Freshly ground black pepper
1   slice stale bread, coarsely chopped
¼   cup chopped walnuts, toasted in a dry skillet

Bring a large pot of salted water to a boil and cook the pasta until just tender. Meanwhile, combine the cream, sherry (if using), and 5 ounces of the Gorgonzola in a medium saucepan or flameproof shallow baking dish and stir constantly over low heat until the cheese is almost melted, about 5 minutes. Drain the pasta, and either return it to its pot and add the cheese sauce or add the pasta directly to the baking dish. Stir over medium-low heat until the sauce thickens slightly, about 2 minutes. Add pepper to taste. If you haven't already, pour the mixture into a shallow baking dish.

Combine the breadcrumbs and nuts and sprinkle the topping over the pasta. Dot with the remaining 1 ounce Gorgonzola. Brown the casserole under a broiler very close to the flame, about 2 minutes.

—MARY PULT AND REBECCA FASTEN

Pappardelle with Shrimp & Zucchini

SERVES 2 TO 3

Strips of zucchini mimic the pasta shape in this light and quick dish.

- 2 medium zucchini, washed and trimmed
- 6 Tablespoons extra-virgin olive oil
- ¾ pound large shrimp, peeled, deveined, rinsed, and patted dry
  Kosher salt and freshly ground black pepper
- 2 cloves garlic, smashed and peeled
- ½ pound dried pappardelle
- ¼ teaspoon crushed red chile flakes
- 2 teaspoons fresh lemon juice
- 15 fresh basil leaves, torn into large pieces
- 2½ ounces thinly sliced prosciutto, cut crosswise into ½-inch-wide strips

Put a large pot of salted water on to boil.

Slice the zucchini into wide strips about ⅛ inch thick, as shown at right.

In a large skillet over high heat, sauté the shrimp, seasoned with salt and pepper, in 1½ tablespoons oil until firm and pink, 2 to 3 minutes. Transfer the shrimp to a plate. Lower the heat to medium, add the remaining 4½ tablespoons oil and the garlic, and cook, swirling the pan, until the garlic browns and the oil is fragrant, 2 to 3 minutes.

Transfer all but 1 tablespoon of the oil to a small bowl. Raise the heat under the skillet to high, add the chile flakes, and pile in the zucchini strips. Season with salt and pepper and sauté until the strips begin to soften (but don't let them turn mushy), 1 to 2 minutes. Discard the garlic cloves.

Boil the pasta until tender. Drain and add to the shrimp, along with the zucchini, lemon juice, and reserved garlic oil. Toss gently. Stir in the basil and the prosciutto and serve immediately.

—TONY ROSENFELD

COOKING RIGHT

Press down hard on a Y-shaped peeler to get nice, thick strips of zucchini. (A mandoline would also work well.) To avoid using the seed-filled core, rotate the zucchini as you peel and discard the core when that's all you are left with.

COOK'S CHOICE

A wider, flat pasta, such as fettucine or tagliatelle would also be wonderful with this sauce.

Linguine with Leeks, Prosciutto & Lemon
SERVES 4

COOKING RIGHT

You want it saucy, not soupy, so add all of the cream and then just enough reserved pasta cooking water to keep things moist.

Trimming the prosciutto fat and rendering it at the start of this dish gives a little extra depth. If your market trims the fat from its prosciutto, just use an extra tablespoon of butter to sauté the leeks.

4 ounces thinly sliced prosciutto, excess fat trimmed and reserved, lean part cut into ¼-inch-wide strips
2 Tablespoons unsalted butter
3 small leeks, white and tender green parts only, sliced (to yield about 2 cups) and well rinsed
   Salt and freshly ground black pepper
   Pinch freshly grated nutmeg
1 cup heavy cream
1 pound dried linguine
1 Tablespoon lemon zest
   Juice of ½ lemon
¾ cup walnuts, roughly chopped and lightly toasted

Bring a large pot of salted water to a boil.

Chop the trimmed prosciutto fat, if using, and put it in a large skillet with the butter. Heat over medium until the butter is melted and the fat is translucent. Add the leeks, season with salt, pepper, and nutmeg, and cover. Cook, stirring occasionally, until tender but not browned, about 10 minutes. Add the prosciutto, stirring to distribute, and then add the cream. Reduce the heat to low and let heat gently, uncovered, while you cook the pasta until just tender. Reserve 1 cup of the pasta cooking water and then drain the pasta, leaving drops of water clinging to it. Add the pasta and half of the reserved pasta cooking water to the skillet. Stir in the lemon zest and juice; season abundantly with black pepper. Heat gently for a few minutes to let the pasta drink up the sauce, adding more pasta cooking water if needed to thin it. Add the walnuts and taste for salt and pepper. Serve immediately.

—MOLLY STEVENS

Cavatelli with Arugula & Ricotta Salata

SERVES 4

If you can't find cavatelli in the dried pasta section of the supermarket, look for it in the freezer section near the ravioli and tortellini.

5   Tablespoons extra-virgin olive oil
¾   cup chopped imported black olives, such as gaeta or kalamata
1   Tablespoon fresh lemon juice
3   large cloves garlic, finely chopped
4½ teaspoons fresh thyme
    Freshly ground black pepper
¼   teaspoon cayenne
1   pound cavatelli
1   large bunch arugula (about 8 ounces), rinsed, dried well, and coarsely chopped
1   cup (about 7 ounces) grated ricotta salata or feta

In a small bowl, whisk together the olive oil, olives, lemon juice, garlic, thyme, black pepper, and cayenne and set aside. Bring a large pot of well-salted water to a boil and cook the cavatelli until al dente. Drain it well and return it to the pan. Add the arugula and the olive-oil mixture, folding gently until the ingredients are combined. Let sit until the arugula has wilted, about 3 minutes. Sprinkle with the ricotta salata just before serving.

—CLIFFORD WRIGHT

COOK'S CHOICE

Ricotta salata is a firm sheep's milk cheese that's lightly salted. You can use feta in its place but soak it in cold water for an hour to lessen its briny flavor.

A "NO COOK" SAUCE MAKES DINNER A BREEZE

In this recipe, the heat from the pasta cooks the sauce, which means there's no extra pot to clean. Here are some other "no cook" pantry staples that when teamed make a great pasta:

- Chopped canned tomatoes, minced garlic, olives, capers, and parsley

- Canned chickpeas, anchovies, chopped canned tomatoes, and prosciutto

- Canned white beans, minced garlic, chopped fresh sage, and Parmigiano Reggiano

Gratin of Polenta with Greens

SERVES 4 AS A FIRST COURSE OR A SIDE DISH

This gratin can be a substantial side dish or a light supper.

1 cup medium-coarse or coarse cornmeal, preferably organic stone-ground

4 cups water

1 teaspoon salt

3 Tablespoons olive oil

1 clove garlic

¼ teaspoon crushed red chile flakes
Freshly ground black pepper

1 pound mixed tender greens, leaves chopped coarsely

⅓ cup grated pecorino romano

Prepare the polenta—Heat the oven to 350°F. In an oiled 3-quart nonstick ovenproof skillet, stir together the cornmeal, water, and salt. Bake uncovered for 40 minutes.

Meanwhile, prepare the greens—In a very large skillet, heat the olive oil over medium-high heat. Add the garlic, chile flakes, and a pinch of black pepper; cook for 1 minute. Pour half the oil into a 1½- or 2-quart ovenproof serving dish, reserving the garlic in the skillet, and then pour another tablespoon into a cup to be drizzled over the final dish. Brush the seasoned oil all over the inside of the serving dish. Add the chopped greens to the oil and garlic remaining in the skillet, cover, and cook over medium heat, stirring occasionally, until wilted and tender, about 10 minutes. Discard the garlic. Season the greens with salt and pepper. Uncover the greens and increase the heat at the end to evaporate any liquid.

When the polenta has cooked 40 minutes, quickly stir in the greens and half the cheese until combined. Taste and add salt if needed. Transfer to the oiled ovenproof serving dish, drizzle with the reserved oil, sprinkle with the remaining cheese, and bake until the cheese is melted, another 10 minutes. Serve hot.

—PAULA WOLFERT

EASY "NO-STIR" POLENTA

Basic Baked Polenta

This basic recipe for baking polenta in the oven rather than cooking it on the stove is adapted from The Polenta Company. It doesn't take less time, but it does take less vigilance (and less stovetop real estate), allowing you to work on the rest of the meal. Some milk with the water will give the polenta a more mellow flavor, but polenta made with all water will keep longer and generally works better if you plan to bake, grill, or fry the polenta.

1 cup medium-coarse or coarse cornmeal

3 to 6 cups water (or half water and half milk), depending on desired consistency (see chart below)

1 Tablespoon butter or olive oil

1 teaspoon salt

Heat the oven to 350°F. Grease a 3-quart, nonstick ovenproof skillet with a little olive oil or butter. Pour in the cornmeal, water, milk (if using), tablespoon of butter or oil, and the salt. Stir with a fork until blended. Bake uncovered for 40 minutes. Stir, taste, add more salt if needed, and bake for another 10 minutes. Remove from the oven and let the polenta rest in the pan for 5 minutes before serving. It will thicken further and firm up as it cools.

Vary polenta's consistency to suit the meal

Here's how you can fiddle with polenta's texture and how to serve it:

CONSISTENCY	HOW TO SERVE	PROPORTIONS
very soft	in a bowl, plain or with toppings	6 parts liquid to 1 part cornmeal
soft	in a bowl, plain or with toppings; as a bed for stews and ragoûts	5 parts liquid to 1 part cornmeal
firm	as a bed for stews and ragoûts; cool and slice into wedges to fry or broil and serve with toppings	4 parts liquid to 1 part cornmeal
very firm	cool and slice into wedges to fry, broil, or grill, and serve with toppings	3 to 3½ parts liquid to 1 part cornmeal

Creamy Goat Cheese Polenta

SERVES 6

Cooking instant polenta with milk and cream gives you a luscious side dish ready in minutes.

1   quart whole milk
2   teaspoons kosher salt
1   cup instant polenta
½   pound fresh goat cheese, crumbled
   Pinch cayenne
½   cup heavy cream
   Freshly ground black pepper

Bring the milk to a boil in a 4-quart saucepan over medium-high heat. Season with 2 teaspoons salt. Slowly whisk in the polenta and cook, stirring constantly, for 5 minutes until the polenta thickens and begins to pull away from the sides of the pan.

Add the goat cheese and cayenne. Whisk until well combined. Whisk in the cream and ½ to 1 cup water to thin the polenta to a porridge-like consistency. Season with salt and pepper.

—ARLENE JACOBS

DRESS UP A BOWL OF POLENTA

You can change the look and flavor with a simple addition.

■ **Add a heavy sprinkling of chopped fresh herbs**—sage is especially good with goat cheese—and drizzle with a little olive oil.

■ **Top with sautéed mushrooms,** chunky tomato sauce, caramelized onions, or roasted vegetables.

■ **Use as a bed for your favorite braisd meat,** such as short ribs or lamb.

Wild Mushroom Risotto

SERVES 2 AS A MAIN COURSE

A little drizzle of white truffle oil right before serving makes this rich risotto even more aromatic and flavorful.

3　cups chicken stock; more if needed

1　ounce dried porcini soaked for 30 minutes in 1 cup warm water; mushrooms chopped, soaking liquid strained and reserved

4　Tablespoons butter

¾　cup arborio rice

2　cups assorted fresh wild mushrooms, cleaned, trimmed, and coarsely chopped

⅔　cup dry white wine
　　Salt

¼　cup chopped flat-leaf parsley

2　Tablespoons freshly grated Parmigiano Reggiano

Heat the chicken stock along with the reserved strained porcini soaking liquid.

In a medium-size, heavy-based saucepan over medium-high heat, melt 2 tablespoons of the butter. Stir in the rice, toasting until it just starts to sizzle and pop, about 1 minute. Stir the porcini and the fresh mushrooms into the rice. Stir in the wine.

When almost all the liquid has disappeared, add just enough hot stock to cover the rice. Lower the heat to maintain a vigorous simmer; stir occasionally. When the stock is almost gone, add enough to cover the rice, along with a pinch of salt. Give the risotto an occasional stir to make sure it isn't sticking to the bottom of the pan and add just enough stock to cover the rice when the liquid has almost disappeared. Continue this way until the rice is al dente, about 20 minutes. Bite into a grain; you should see a white pin-dot in the center. Take the risotto off the heat. Add the remaining 2 tablespoons butter; stir vigorously for a few seconds. Add the parsley, cheese, and more salt if needed. Stir in more stock to loosen the risotto, if you like. Serve immediately.　　—ALAN TARDI

COOKING RIGHT

When the pan looks this dry, it's time to add more stock. But don't flood the rice, add a little at a time so the rice can absorb the liquid.

COOKING RIGHT

Toasting the rice keeps it from getting mushy. Let it cook for a full minute—that's longer than you think—but don't let it brown.

Risotto of Sweet Sausage & Broccoli Raab

SERVES 2 AS A MAIN COURSE

Use a good, mild sausage and break it up so the pieces don't overwhelm the rice.

2   Tablespoons butter
½   cup arborio rice
¼   pound sweet Italian sausage, skinned and crumbled
1   small clove garlic, chopped
½   cup dry white wine
3   to 3½ cups chicken stock brought to a simmer on the stove
    Salt
    Pinch cayenne
¼   pound broccoli raab, boiled for 5 minutes, drained, squeezed dry, and coarsely chopped
    Freshly ground black pepper
2   Tablespoons freshly grated Parmigiano Reggiano

In a large, heavy-based saucepan over medium-high heat, melt the butter. Stir in the rice, toasting until it just starts to sizzle and pop, about 1 minute. Add the sausage and garlic. Stir, breaking up the meat into small bits, until the sausage has lost its pink color, about 1 minute. Pour in the wine. Stir occasionally, cooking until the liquid is almost gone, about 2 minutes. Add just enough hot stock to cover the rice. Lower the heat to maintain a vigorous simmer; stir occasionally.

When the liquid is almost gone, add just enough hot stock to cover the rice, along with a pinch of salt and cayenne. Give the risotto an occasional stir to make sure it isn't sticking to the bottom of the pan and add just enough stock to cover the rice when the liquid has almost disappeared. After a couple of additions of stock, add the broccoli raab. Continue adding stock and checking until the rice is al dente, about 20 minutes. Bite into a grain; you should see a small white pin-dot in the center. Take the risotto off the heat and stir vigorously for a few seconds. Fold in the pepper, cheese, and a pinch of salt if needed. Stir in a few tablespoons of stock to loosen the risotto, if you like. Serve immediately.

—ALAN TARDI

MAKE RICE CAKES WITH LEFTOVER RISOTTO

Leftover risotto makes delicious *tortine de riso*. Simply shape cooled risotto into cakes about ¾ inch thick and sauté them in olive oil until browned on both sides. If you want to get fancy, bread the cakes before frying.

Risotto with Corn, Tomatoes & Basil

SERVES 3 AS A MAIN DISH; 6 AS A SIDE DISH

Cooking the corn in the same pot as the risotto saves a step and adds flavor.

4 cups low-salt chicken broth
3 ears corn, shucked and cleaned of any silk
2 Tablespoons unsalted butter
1 shallot, finely chopped
1 cup arborio rice
⅓ cup dry white wine
1 cup chopped plum or cherry tomatoes
2 teaspoons extra-virgin olive oil
3 Tablespoons torn fresh basil leaves
   Kosher salt and freshly ground black pepper
⅓ cup freshly grated Parmigiano Reggiano

Heat the broth in a pot large enough to fit the corn to just below a simmer. Add the corn, simmer for 4 minutes, and transfer to a plate; reserve the broth and keep it hot. Slice the kernels off the cob.

In a heavy-based deep skillet or wide saucepan, melt the butter over medium heat. Add the shallot and cook, stirring until it's translucent, about 2 minutes. Add the rice and stir until the grains are well coated with butter or oil. Pour in the wine, stir, and cook until the wine is absorbed, about 1 minute. Ladle in about 1½ cups of the broth and cook, stirring occasionally, until absorbed. Continue adding broth in ½-cup increments, stirring and simmering until it's absorbed each time.

While the rice is simmering, combine the tomatoes, extra-virgin olive oil, and 2 tablespoons of the basil in a small bowl. Season with salt and pepper and set aside.

When the rice is just barely tender, stir in the corn. Cook the rice until creamy but still firm to the tooth, 20 to 25 minutes total. Remove from the heat, fold in the Parmigiano and then the tomato mixture. Top each serving with the remaining basil and serve.

—MOLLY STEVENS

CHICKEN

If you're looking for a fresh take on chicken, you're in luck. Here are recipes that combine the best of what's familiar—sautéed chicken cutlets, roast chicken, chicken stew—with exciting flavor combinations: a chile-cinnamon rub, a balsamic-orange glaze, a yogurt and ginger marinade. You'll also find brilliant yet easy techniques that you can use to create your own new chicken dishes as well as contemporary takes on turkey.

THE RECIPES

Parmesan-Crumbed Chicken

Chicken Breasts Stuffed with Olives & Goat Cheese

Tandoori-Style Chicken

Quick Chicken Sauté with Snow Peas & Cilantro

Broiled Chicken Thighs with Coriander Rub

Seared Chicken Breast with Quick Pan Sauce

Southwestern Spiced Chicken & Black Bean Stew

Sweet & Spicy Sticky Chicken

Grilled Coffee-Brined Chicken Breasts

Glazed Balsamic-Orange Chicken

Braised Chicken with Capers, Tomatoes & Parsley

Butterflied Roast Chicken with Chile-Cinnamon Rub

Crisp Panko Chicken Cutlets

Turkey Cutlets with Mustard Cream Sauce

Seared Turkey & White Bean Burgers

Truffle-Scented Cornish Game Hens with Prosciutto & Wild Mushrooms

COOKING AHEAD

You can coat the chicken up to an hour before cooking it. Take the coated breasts out of the refrigerator about 10 minutes before roasting them.

Parmesan-Crumbed Chicken

SERVES 6

There's no need to pan-fry for a crisp coating; simply bake these breasts in a hot oven.

Using one hand, lay a marinated chicken breast on the crumbs.

Use your other hand to scoop and pat the crumbs on the breast to give both sides an even coating. Put the coated breast on the baking sheet.

6   boneless, skinless chicken breast halves
6   Tablespons Dijon mustard
1   Tablespoon white wine or water
¾   teaspoon salt
¼   teaspoon freshly ground black pepper
1   cup freshly grated Parmesan
1   cup fresh English muffin (or sandwich bread) crumbs
    Freshly ground black pepper
4   Tablespoons melted butter

Rinse the breasts and pat them dry. In a shallow bowl, whisk together the mustard, wine, salt, and pepper and add the chicken.

In a large shallow dish, mix the cheese, breadcrumbs, and pepper. Drizzle the melted butter over the crumb mixture and toss until well combined.

Heat the oven to 450°F and butter a baking sheet or rack. Follow the directions in the photos at left for coating the chicken. Roast the chicken until it's crisp, browned, and cooked through, 25 to 30 minutes. Check after 15 minutes. If the chicken is getting too brown, reduce the heat to 400° and add 5 minutes to the total cooking time.

—ELIZABETH TERRY

Chicken Breasts Stuffed with Olives & Goat Cheese

SERVES 4

Partially covering the chicken breasts during cooking keeps them moist and juicy.

- 3 ounces fresh goat cheese
- 1 Tablespoon milk
- 1 clove garlic, minced
- 1 Tablespoon chopped flat-leaf parsley
  Pinch crumbled dried oregano
  Pinch dried chile flakes
- 1 Tablespoon chopped kalamata or other
  good-quality black olives
  Salt and freshly ground black pepper
- 4 boneless, skinless chicken breast halves
- 2 Tablespoons olive oil
- ½ cup dry white wine

In a small bowl, mash the goat cheese and milk together until smooth. Mix in the garlic, parsley, oregano, and chile flakes. Stir in the olives and season with salt and pepper.

On the thickest side of each breast, cut a deep, 3-inch-long pocket and stuff the goat cheese mixture into each pocket. Close by pressing the flesh together, securing with a toothpick if necessary.

In a large frying pan, heat the oil over medium-high heat. Have ready a lid that's too small for the pan but will cover all the breasts. Cook the chicken on one side until golden brown, 5 to 6 minutes. Turn the breasts over, season with salt and pepper, set the lid on top of them, and cook until the chicken is done, about another 10 minutes.

Transfer the chicken to a warm serving plate. Pour the wine into the pan and cook, scraping up the flavorful brown bits stuck to the pan, until reduced to a glossy syrup. Drizzle the reduction over the chicken and serve.

—JOANNE WEIR

COOK'S CHOICE

Try some sun-dried tomatoes added to (or in place of) the olives. In the summer, flavor the goat cheese with fresh herbs such as basil, chives, and mint.

Tandoori-Style Chicken

SERVES 4 TO 6

In this recipe, a hot grill replicates the intense heat of a traditional tandoor oven. Serve the chicken with some fragrant basmati rice and peas and spoon the flavorful juices that accumulate on the platter over the chicken.

For the marinade:

1 2-inch piece ginger, peeled
4 large cloves garlic
¼ teaspoon turmeric
1 teaspoon chili powder
1½ teaspoons salt
½ teaspoon cumin seeds, ground
¾ cup plain low-fat yogurt
1 Tablespoon fresh lime juice

For the chicken:

2 to 3 pounds boneless chicken thighs and breasts
¼ cup melted butter or olive oil

For the garnish:

½ mild onion, thinly sliced
½ cup chopped cilantro leaves
1 or 2 fresh green chiles, thinly sliced
1 lime, cut in wedges

Make the marinade—In a blender or food processor, blend the ginger and garlic to a fine paste (you may need to add a little water to make a paste). Add the turmeric, chili powder, salt, cumin, yogurt, and lime juice; process until combined.

Prepare the chicken—Remove the skin from the chicken, leaving some fat. Make a few slits in each piece and transfer to a nonreactive dish large enough for the pieces to lie flat. Pour the marinade over the chicken and stir to coat the chicken thoroughly. Seal with plastic, refrigerate, and marinate for at least 4 to no more than 12 hours, turning the chicken once.

COOKING RIGHT

Slit the chicken in a few places to help the full—not spicy—flavors of the yogurt-based marinade permeate the meat.

Grill the chicken—Ready a charcoal grill with an even layer of coals, or heat a gas grill to high. While the grill is heating up, take the chicken out of the refrigerator. When the charcoal is red-hot, lay the chicken pieces on the grill about 2 inches apart. Baste with any remaining marinade. Cover the grill, leaving the vents half-open.

After about 5 minutes, remove the grill lid and turn over the chicken pieces; they should look slightly charred. Replace the lid and continue cooking for another 5 to 7 minutes. Uncover the chicken, baste it with the melted butter, turn it over, and leave it uncovered for the rest of the cooking time. Baste after 2 or 3 minutes and test for doneness: The meat should feel firm when you press it.

Transfer the chicken to a large platter. Arrange the onion, cilantro, chiles, and lime wedges over the chicken and seal the platter with foil. Let the chicken rest for 10 minutes to absorb the garnish flavors.

—LEONA PRIYA DALAVAI

COOKING RIGHT

Start testing for doneness after the minimum cooking time, and pull the chicken off the grill as soon as it feels tender.

Quick Chicken Sauté with Snow Peas & Cilantro

SERVES 2

If you have some bean sprouts on hand, add them to the dish for a little extra crunch.

For a golden crust (and less sticking), let the chicken sit undisturbed for one minute in the pan before turning.

Take the chicken out of the pan while it's still faintly pink in the center; it will continue to cook off of the heat but won't dry out.

2 boneless, skinless chicken breast halves (12 ounces total), cut into ¾-inch chunks Kosher salt and freshly ground black pepper

2 teaspoons cornstarch

¼ cup water or homemade or low-salt canned chicken broth

2 Tablespoons peanut or vegetable oil

5 ounces fresh snow peas, trimmed

1 1-inch chunk fresh ginger, peeled and cut into thin matchsticks

1 clove garlic, minced

¼ cup sake or mirin (sweet rice wine)

3 Tablespoons soy sauce

2 Tablespoons rice-wine vinegar

1 Tablespoon honey Cilantro for garnish

Season the chicken with salt and pepper. In a small bowl, blend the cornstarch into the water or broth. Heat 2 teaspoons of the oil in a sauté pan over medium-high heat. Add the snow peas and cook, stirring, until slightly browned, 2 to 3 minutes. Transfer to a bowl. Heat another 1 tablespoon oil, add the chicken, and cook for 1 minute. Turn the chicken over and cook, turning it occasionally, 3 to 5 minutes. Add the chicken to the peas.

Heat the remaining 1 teaspoon oil in the pan. Add the ginger and cook about 1 minute. Reduce the heat to medium, add the garlic, and cook about 30 seconds. Add the sake, soy sauce, vinegar, honey, and the cornstarch mixture and stir, scraping up any browned bits. Bring to a boil, reduce the heat to medium low, and add the chicken and snow peas. Toss, season with salt and pepper, sprinkle with cilantro, and serve.

—MARYELLEN DRISCOLL

Broiled Chicken Thighs with Coriander Rub

SERVES 4

For a fuller, more fragrant coriander flavor, grind whole coriander seeds yourself in a spice grinder or an electric coffee grinder dedicated to spices.

8 boneless, skinless chicken thighs, trimmed of excess fat
   Vegetable oil for coating
   Salt and freshly ground black pepper
1 Tablespoon ground coriander
2 Tablespoons fish sauce
2 teaspoons light brown sugar
¼ lime
¼ cup thinly sliced scallion greens

Adjust the oven rack to the position closest to the broiler and set the broiler on high. Coat both sides of each thigh with just enough oil to get the seasonings to stick. Sprinkle each side with salt, pepper, and a portion of the coriander, rubbing the seasonings into the meat. Mix the fish sauce and sugar in a small bowl; set aside.

Lay the thighs flat on a broiler pan and broil until they're opaque on top, 3 to 4 minutes. Remove the thighs from the oven. Without turning them, brush them with the fish sauce mixture and return them to the oven. Continue to broil until the thighs are spotty brown and cooked through, another 4 to 5 minutes. Transfer to a serving plate; pour the pan juices over the chicken. Squeeze lime juice over the chicken and sprinkle with the scallions.

—PAM ANDERSON

Seared Chicken Breast with Quick Pan Sauce

SERVES 4

*This technique and the accompanying sauces also would work well
with turkey cutlets, boneless pork chops, or sliced pork loin.*

4   trimmed boneless, skinless chicken breasts, tenderloin removed
    and cooked separately or saved for another use
    Kosher salt and freshly ground black pepper
    Flour for dredging
    Ingredients for pan sauce (see the recipes on the facing page)
3   Tablespoons unsalted butter
1   Tablespoon vegetable or olive oil

Season the chicken breasts on both sides with ample salt and pepper. Put
a handful of flour in a pie pan or other sided plate and position it near
the stove. Combine the sauce ingredients of your choice in a 1-cup Pyrex
measuring cup or small bowl.

Heat 2 tablespoons of the butter and the oil in a large skillet over medium
heat. Dredge one of the chicken breasts in the flour, coating both sides well
but shaking off any excess. Increase the heat of the pan to medium high.

Before adding the chicken, test the heat of the pan by flicking in a little
of the dredging flour. If the flour sizzles enthusiastically and immediately
turns golden, the pan is ready. Add the first floured chicken breast. Then
quickly flour the remaining breasts and add them to the pan. Cook for
about 4 minutes without moving the breasts. Then, starting with the first
one in the pan, turn them over and cook for another 3 or 4 minutes on
the other side.

Transfer the chicken to a plate or plates and keep it warm. Add the pan
sauce ingredients to the hot pan and boil, stirring and scraping up the
browned bits in the bottom of the pan, over high heat until the liquid is
reduced by half. Add the remaining tablespoon of butter and whisk until
smooth and glossy. (Tilt the pan to bring the small amount of liquid to
one side while you whisk in the butter.) Spoon the sauce over the chicken
and serve immediately.

—PAM ANDERSON

COOKING RIGHT

Choose the right size skillet so
that the cutlets have neither too
much nor too little space between
them. A 12-inch pan works best for
four cutlets.

QUICK PAN SAUCES

These sauces are designed for 4 chicken breasts, yielding about 1 to 1½ tablespoons of sauce per breast. If you decide you want a bit more sauce, increase the total liquid ingredients to ⅔ cup and whisk in a little more butter.

Red Wine and Mustard

- ¼ cup low-salt chicken stock
- ¼ cup red wine
- 1 teaspoon Dijon mustard

Curried Chutney

- 6 Tablespoons low-salt chicken stock
- 2 Tablespoons rice wine vinegar
- 2 Tablespoons prepared chutney
- ¼ teaspoon curry powder

Orange-Dijon

- ½ cup orange juice
- 1 teaspoon Dijon mustard
- ½ teaspoon minced fresh rosemary
- 1 Tablespoon brown sugar

Port with Dried Cherries

- ½ cup port wine
- 2 Tablespoons dried cherries or cranberries
- 2 teaspoons seedless raspberry jam

Lemon-Caper

- 6 Tablespoons low-salt chicken stock
- 2 Tablespoons lemon juice
- 2 teaspoons drained capers

Vermouth with Prunes

- 6 Tablespoons sweet vermouth
- 2 Tablespoons cider vinegar
- ¼ cup chopped prunes

Tomato-Tarragon

- ¼ cup low-salt chicken stock
- ¼ cup dry white wine
- 1 teaspoon minced fresh tarragon
- 4 canned tomatoes, seeded and chopped

Add the flavorings to the hot pan.

Scrape up those yummy stuck-on bits and reduce the liquid by half.

Pour the sauce over the chicken and serve immediately.

COOKING RIGHT

For the best browning, cook the thighs in batches, leaving room between them in the pan.

Southwestern Spiced Chicken & Black Bean Stew

SERVES 4 TO 6

A dried chipotle gives the broth a wonderful smoky spice, but the stew is excellent without it if you can't find chipotles at your market.

2 Tablespoons extra-virgin olive oil

3 thick slices bacon

6 skinless, bone-in chicken thighs, large pieces of fat trimmed
   Kosher salt and freshly ground black pepper

1 large yellow onion, diced

1 red bell pepper, cored, seeded, and finely diced

2 teaspoons chile powder

1 teaspoon ground cumin

¾ cup beer

1 can (15½ ounces) black beans, rinsed (about 2 cups)

1 dried chipotle (optional)

2 cups homemade or low-salt canned chicken broth; more if needed

3 Tablespoons chopped fresh cilantro leaves

1 lime
   Sour cream for garnish
   Fried tortilla strips (optional; see p. 50)

Heat the oil in a large Dutch oven or heavy pot over medium heat. Add the bacon and cook until it renders much of its fat and crisps slightly, about 7 minutes. Transfer the bacon to a plate lined with paper towels. Season the chicken well with salt and pepper. Add half of the thighs to the pot and brown them well on both sides, 2 to 3 minutes per side. Transfer to a plate. Brown the remaining thighs and reserve with the rest.

Add the onion and bell pepper to the pot, season well with salt, and cook, stirring often, until the onion softens and browns slightly, about 7 minutes. Raise the heat to high, add the chile powder and cumin, and cook, stirring, for 30 seconds. Add the beer and cook until it's almost completely reduced, about 3 minutes. Add the beans, the chipotle (if using), and the chicken broth. Bring to a boil, reduce to a simmer, and

COOK'S CHOICE

The fried tortilla strips are optional, but they add a fun, crunchy contrast.

cook for 5 minutes. Transfer 2 cups of the beans and broth (but not the chipotle) to a blender, purée, and then mix it back into the rest of the broth.

Return the thighs to the pot, cover with the lid slightly ajar, and simmer until the chicken is cooked through, about 30 minutes. If the stew is too thick, thin it with more chicken broth. Discard the chipotle. Crumble the reserved bacon. Juice one half of the lime; cut the other half into wedges. Stir the bacon, lime juice, and 2 tablespoons of the cilantro into the stew and season well with salt and pepper. Serve immediately, ladling some of the beans and chicken into each bowl. Sprinkle each serving with the remaining cilantro and a small dollop of sour cream. Serve with the lime wedges and fried tortilla strips, if you like.

—TONY ROSENFELD

THREE STEPS TO A SHORTCUT STEW

The following steps give this stew (and all similarly prepared stews) the intense flavor and thick texture that normally only come from long cooking.

1 Brown the chicken thighs to add a rich caramelized flavor.

2 Purée the cooked vegetables to give the liquid a silky smooth "stewy" texture.

3 Finish cooking the chicken in the sauce so flavors mingle.

Sweet & Spicy Sticky Chicken

SERVES 4

This dish, full of Asian flavors, is best served with plenty of steamed jasmine rice and sautéed snap peas. Look for fish sauce in the Asian section of your grocery store or at an Asian market.

½ cup dark brown sugar

¼ cup fish sauce

⅓ cup water

3 Tablespoons rice-wine vinegar

2 Tablespoons soy sauce

1 Tablespoon minced fresh ginger

1 clove garlic, minced

½ teaspoon freshly ground black pepper

½ teaspoon crushed red chile flakes

1 Tablespoon peanut or vegetable oil

3 scallions (white and green parts), thinly sliced

8 chicken thighs (bone in or boneless), fat and skin removed
Cilantro sprigs as a garnish

In a bowl, whisk together the brown sugar, fish sauce, water, rice-wine vinegar, soy sauce, ginger, garlic, black pepper, and crushed red chile flakes.

Heat the oil in a large frying pan over medium heat. Add the scallions and cook until soft, about 3 minutes. Add the thighs and the brown sugar mixture. Turn the heat to high and bring to a boil. As soon as it comes to a boil, reduce the heat to low and simmer, turning the thighs occasionally, until cooked, 25 to 30 minutes.

Remove the thighs from the pan and cover with foil to keep warm. Increase the heat to high and reduce the sauce by half or until it is slightly thickened and resembles a bubbling caramel sauce. Serve the chicken with the sauce, garnished with the cilantro sprigs.

—JOANNE WEIR

COOK'S CHOICE

Use boneless or bone-in thighs. If you prefer to bone your own thighs, use a sharp knife and follow the contours of the bone, keeping the blade close to it.

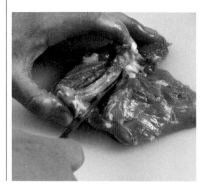

Grilled Coffee-Brined Chicken Breasts

SERVES 4

Serve the chicken with your favorite barbecue sauce, if you like, and some corn on the cob.

¼ cup kosher salt

¼ cup packed dark brown sugar

3 cups water

4 slices lemon (¼ inch thick)

1 Tablespoon black peppercorns

1 Tablespoon mustard seeds

1 Tablespoon coriander seeds

¾ cup strong brewed coffee

4 boneless, skinless chicken breast halves, trimmed and rinsed

1 cup wood chips (such as oak or hickory), soaked in water for 1 hour and drained (optional)

2 Tablespoons melted butter or olive oil

COOKING AHEAD

The chicken needs to soak for at least 2 hours in the coffee-flavored brine. The pay-off: a subtle toasty flavor and an attractive mocha hue.

To make the brine, combine the salt, sugar, water, lemon, peppercorns, mustard seeds, and coriander seeds in a medium saucepan and heat over medium heat, whisking occasionally, until the salt and sugar dissolve, about 5 minutes. Transfer to a medium-large bowl, add the coffee, and refrigerate until cool, about 15 minutes. Put the chicken breasts in the brine and set a pot lid or small plate on top to keep them submerged. Refrigerate them in the brine for 2 to 3 hours.

Heat a gas grill to high or prepare a hot charcoal fire with wood chips, if using.

Drain the chicken and blot dry with paper towels. Lightly brush both sides with the melted butter or oil. Arrange the breasts on the grill at a 45-degree angle to the bars of the grate. Grill until they have grill marks, about 2 minutes, and then rotate them 90 degrees (to get a crosshatch of grill marks) and continue grilling for 2 to 4 minutes. Flip the breasts and cook until they're firm to the touch, another 4 to 6 minutes. Serve immediately.

—STEVEN RAICHLEN

Glazed Balsamic-Orange Chicken

SERVES 4

To make a flavorful, colorful side dish for this chicken, toss some cooked orzo with olive oil, garlic, greens, toasted pine nuts, and a splash of balsamic vinegar.

COOKING RIGHT

A flash under the broiler crisps the skin. For even browning, rotate the pieces.

¾ cup fresh orange juice
3 Tablespoons dark brown sugar
2 Tablespoons balsamic vinegar
2 teaspoons dry mustard
1 Tablespoon chopped fresh thyme
1 3- to 4-pound roasting chicken, cut into pieces (or 3½ pounds chicken pieces), rinsed and dried
    Salt and freshly ground black pepper

Set a rack at the highest oven position. Heat the oven to 400°F. In a small saucepan, combine the orange juice and brown sugar. Boil until reduced by half. Stir in the balsamic vinegar, dry mustard, and thyme. Pour into a small, shallow bowl; mix until smooth. Dredge each chicken piece in the glaze, coating completely. Put the pieces, skin side down, in a rimmed, shallow 10x15-inch sheet pan. Pour any leftover glaze over the chicken; sprinkle liberally with salt and pepper. Roast on the top rack until the juices run barely clear when you prick the chicken, about 40 minutes. Remove the pan from the oven and set the broiler on high. Turn the chicken over and baste it with the pan drippings. If a lot of fat has rendered out, spoon some off before broiling to prevent flare-ups. Broil, basting the chicken and rotating the pieces for even browning, until the chicken pieces are shiny and well browned, about 8 minutes. Drizzle the chicken with the pan drippings before serving.

—MIMA LECOCQ

Braised Chicken with Capers, Tomatoes & Parsley

SERVES 4 TO 6

Serve polenta, pasta, or even a crusty peasant bread to soak up the tangy sauce the short braise creates.

- 3 pounds chicken pieces
  Salt and freshly ground black pepper
  Flour for dredging
- 3 Tablespoons extra-virgin olive oil
- 1 cup dry white wine
- 4 cloves garlic, crushed or minced
- 1 cup coarsely chopped onion
- 2 pounds fresh tomatoes, peeled, seeded, excess juice removed, and chopped, or 2 cans (28 ounces each) of peeled plum tomatoes, well drained, seeded, and chopped (3 cups)
- ½ cup drained large capers
- ⅓ cup finely chopped flat-leaf parsley

Season the chicken with salt and pepper. Dredge it in the flour, shaking off any excess. Pour a scant ⅛ inch olive oil into a large, heavy skillet and heat the oil until it's almost smoking. Brown the chicken in one uncrowded layer on one side, about 5 minutes, and then turn to brown the other side. Transfer to a platter.

Pour off excess fat from the pan, add the wine, and deglaze over high heat, using a wooden spoon to dislodge any browned bits clinging to the pan. Simmer 1 minute. Add the garlic and onion and cook over moderate heat until tender, stirring occasionally, 5 to 7 minutes.

Stir in the tomatoes and return the chicken and any juices to the pan. Cook, covered, over medium-low heat, until the chicken is tender when pierced with a knife, about 40 minutes. Transfer the chicken to a warm serving platter. Boil the sauce over high heat until slightly reduced. Stir in the capers, taste, and adjust seasonings. Pour the sauce over the chicken, garnish with the parsley, and serve.

—ROBERT WEMISCHNER

COOKING RIGHT

Capers often need a rinse before using. But this dish benefits from draining—but not rinsing—brined capers so they contribute maximum flavor.

Butterflied Roast Chicken with Chile-Cinnamon Rub

SERVES 2 TO 3

Butterflying the chicken makes it cook faster and also creates lots of crisp skin.

 2 Tablespoons olive oil

 2 teaspoons minced garlic

10 sprigs fresh thyme or 4 sprigs fresh rosemary; more for garnish

 1 teaspoon pure chile powder or ½ teaspoon cayenne

 ½ teaspoon ground cinnamon

 1 teaspoon paprika

 1 teaspoon ground cumin

 1 teaspoon ground coriander seeds

 1 teaspoon coarse salt

 ½ teaspoon sugar, preferably granulated brown

 1 chicken (3½ pounds) rinsed inside and out and patted dry with paper towels

Heat the oven to 475°F.

Pour the olive oil into a small saucepan and add the minced garlic and the thyme or rosemary. Set the pan over high heat until the oil is hot,

about 30 seconds. Reduce the heat to low and cook until the garlic has browned slightly, about 3 minutes. Remove from the heat and let infuse for at least 10 minutes or up to 2 hours.

In a small bowl, mix together the chile powder, cinnamon, paprika, cumin, coriander, salt, and sugar.

Set the chicken on a board, breast side down, and butterfly it as shown in the photos at right.

Set the chicken skin side down in a shallow roasting pan or a baking sheet. Brush thoroughly with half of the garlic olive oil (use the herb sprigs as a brush, if you want, before discarding them) and sprinkle with half of the spice rub. Turn the bird over and gently loosen the skin over the breast and thighs. Brush the remaining oil and most of the spice rub directly on the flesh under the skin. Rub the remaining spices on the skin. Pierce the skin with a sharp fork or small paring knife randomly in about 10 places to help it crisp.

Roast until the skin is nicely browned and the thigh meat is 170°F or the juices run clear, about 40 minutes. Remove the chicken from the oven, tent with foil, and let rest for 10 minutes.

To serve, halve the chicken by cutting straight down the center of the breastbone. Carve each half into drumsticks, thighs, wings, and breast, and garnish on a platter with fresh thyme or rosemary, if you like.

—STEPHEN PYLES

SPLIT AND THEN FLATTEN

Using poultry shears, remove the narrow backbone starting at the neck. Cut through the ribs, but leave the breastbone intact. Turn the bird over.

Firmly press the breast with the heel of your hand to make the bird lie flat—you'll need to break the collar bone and some ribs. Tuck the wing tips behind the shoulder.

Crisp Panko Chicken Cutlets

SERVES 4

These light, crisp chicken cutlets taste just great on their own, but you also can serve them with a flavored mayonnaise, a garlicky aïoli, a little marinara, or your favorite dipping sauce.

COOKING RIGHT

For the crispiest cutlet, use Japanese-style breadcrumbs. Called panko flakes or panko crumbs, they're available at Asian markets and in the Asian section of some supermarkets. With their irregular shape and dry, coarse texture, panko crumbs seem to absorb less oil and stay crisp longer than regular crumbs. They also make a great topping for casseroles.

4   boneless, skinless chicken breast halves
    Kosher salt and black pepper
½   cup all-purpose flour
3   eggs, lightly beaten with ⅓ cup water
2   cups panko crumbs
    Vegetable oil for frying

If the tenderloins are still attached to the chicken breasts, remove them and bread and fry them separately, or save them for another use. With a sharp knife, lightly score both sides of the chicken breasts in a checkerboard pattern. Lay a sheet of plastic wrap over the breasts and pound until they're about ½ inch thick. Season with salt and pepper.

Dredge the chicken in the flour and then dip it in the beaten eggs, shaking to remove excess. Dip each piece in the flour and egg again and then coat the chicken in the panko.

In a deep, straight-sided sauté pan, heat about ¼ inch vegetable oil over medium high until the oil ripples and shimmers in the pan and instantly erupts into lots of bubbles when you dip a corner of a chicken breast into it. Immediately reduce the heat to medium low and fry the chicken in batches until cooked through and golden brown on both sides, 4 to 6 minutes per side. If the oil seems to cool down too much during frying, increase the heat a little to maintain a steady bubbling action. Drain the chicken on paper towels and serve.

—HIROKO SHIMBO

Turkey Cutlets with Mustard Cream Sauce
SERVES 4

Sautéed spinach makes a great bed for the cutlet and pairs well with the mustard sauce.

1½ pounds turkey breast cutlets (about 10 pieces, each ¼ inch thick)
   Kosher salt and freshly ground black pepper
¼ cup olive oil
1 large shallot, finely chopped (about 2 Tablespoons)
1 teaspoon minced fresh garlic (about 2 small cloves)
¾ cup homemade or low-salt canned chicken broth
¼ cup heavy cream
1 Tablespoon grainy mustard
10 ounces fresh spinach (about 6 cups), washed and stemmed
2 teaspoons fresh lemon juice
2 Tablespoons finely chopped fresh flat-leaf parsley (optional)

COOKING RIGHT

If you can't find turkey cutlets, buy a boneless turkey breast and cut it on the diagonal into ¼-inch slices.

Season the turkey with salt and pepper. Heat 2 tablespoons of the oil in a large skillet over medium-high heat. When it's hot, brown the turkey (working in batches so the turkey is evenly spaced) until it's cooked through, 1 to 2 minutes per side. Transfer the cooked turkey to a wide plate and cover loosely with foil. Reduce the heat to low and add 1 tablespoon olive oil. Add the shallot and sauté, stirring frequently, until it softens slightly, about 3 minutes. Add ½ teaspoon of the garlic and sauté, stirring, another 30 seconds. Increase the heat to high, add the broth and cook until it reduces by half, about 5 minutes. Add the cream and mustard and cook 1 to 2 minutes, whisking until thickened. Season with salt and pepper; set aside.

Heat the remaining 1 tablespoon oil in another large skillet over medium-high heat. When it's hot, add the remaining ½ teaspoon garlic. Sauté for 15 seconds, shaking the pan so the garlic doesn't burn. Add the spinach and cover the pan. Cook, stirring occasionally, until the spinach wilts completely, about 2 minutes. Toss with the lemon juice and remove from the heat.

Serve immediately, putting some spinach in the middle of each plate, topped with a portion of the turkey, a spoonful of the sauce, and a sprinkling of parsley.

—JENNIFER BUSHMAN

Seared Turkey & White Bean Burgers

YIELDS 4 SMALL BURGERS; SERVES 2 TO 4

Top these burgers with tomato and thinly sliced red onion.
In place of ketchup, try a tangy honey mustard.

½ cup canned small white beans (cannellini are also fine),
   rinsed and drained
3 Tablespoons olive oil
½ clove garlic, minced
2 Tablespoons finely diced red bell pepper
3 Tablespoons plain dried breadcrumbs
1½ teaspoons Worcestershire sauce
1 large egg
1 Tablespoon thinly sliced chives
½ pound ground turkey
   Kosher salt and freshly ground black pepper
8 slices (½ inch thick) good country bread (like ciabatta), toasted

COOK'S CHOICE

You can grind your own turkey
breast if you like. Cut the meat
into cubes and pulse in the food
processor.

Combine the white beans, 1 tablespoon of the olive oil, and the garlic in a large bowl. Using a fork, lightly smash the beans and mix with the oil and garlic until blended. Add the red pepper, breadcrumbs, Worcestershire sauce, egg, and chives. Mix until blended. Crumble the ground turkey and add it to the bowl, along with ½ teaspoon salt and a generous sprinkling of pepper. Gently mix with a fork or your hands until just blended; don't overmix or the burgers will be tough. Fill a medium bowl with water, moisten your hands, and shape the meat into four patties about 3 inches in diameter and ¾ inch thick.

Heat the remaining 2 tablespoons olive oil in a large nonstick skillet over medium heat. Cook the burgers until the bottoms are browned, 4 to 5 minutes. Flip the burgers and continue cooking until they're firm to the touch and register 165°F on an instant-read thermometer, another 5 to 8 minutes. Serve immediately on the toasted bread.

—ABIGAIL JOHNSON DODGE

Truffle-Scented Cornish Game Hens with Prosciutto & Wild Mushrooms

SERVES 6

Earthy mushrooms and heady truffle oil make this dish a standout. For the wild mushrooms, use a mix of chanterelles, porcini, and morels.

6   Cornish game hens (about 1½ pounds each), neck and giblets removed and discarded or saved for stock, hens rinsed and patted dry
    Salt and freshly ground black pepper
3   Tablespoons unsalted butter
¾   pound fresh wild mushrooms, finely chopped
1½ teaspoons chopped fresh thyme
3   thin slices prosciutto (2 ounces total) cut into ¼-inch dice
3   Tablespoons white truffle oil

Season the cavity of each hen with salt and pepper. In a large skillet over medium heat, melt 1 tablespoon of the butter. Add the mushrooms and season with salt and pepper. Add the thyme and cook, stirring occasionally, until the mushrooms are soft and the juices have evaporated, 5 to 8 minutes. Transfer to a bowl to cool. Stir in the prosciutto and truffle oil.

Heat the oven to 425°F. Insert your fingertips at the wing end of the breast and gently loosen the skin over the breast and around the legs. Divide the stuffing into six equal portions. Place one portion of the stuffing under the skin and with your fingers, distribute it evenly over the breast and thigh. With kitchen twine, tie the legs together. Tuck the wings underneath. Repeat with each hen.

Arrange the birds breast side up on a wire rack set in a shallow roasting pan (or two). Melt the remaining 2 tablespoons butter and use half to brush over the hens. Season each hen with salt and pepper. Roast for 20 minutes and brush with the remaining melted butter. Roast until the juices run clear when you prick the thickest part of the thigh and an instant-read thermometer inserted in the thigh registers 170°F, another 25 to 30 minutes. Transfer the hens to a platter, tent with foil, and let stand for 10 minutes before serving.

—JOANNE WEIR

COOKING RIGHT

Keep the stuffing under wraps by buying hens with their skin intact (no tears) and working gently (watch those fingernails) as you ease the mushroom stuffing under the skin.

BEEF, PORK & LAMB

The funny thing about what's "new" in cooking is that it's often a rediscovery of something "old." Take braising, which has recently become exceedingly popular with both restaurant chefs and home cooks. You'll find plenty of braises here, but also many quick-cooking dishes, such as a spicy grilled flank steak and tender glazed pork tenderloin.

THE RECIPES

COOKING RIGHT

Trimming arugula is a snap. Simply twist off the thick stems and the leaves are ready to go.

Sliced Steak with Rosemary, Lemon & Arugula
SERVES 2

To capture all the great juices from the beef that mingle with the lemon juice and arugula, serve this dish—still sizzling—in the same pan it's cooked in. Fajita pans, small paella pans, and enameled cast-iron gratin pans will go from stove to table. It's best to cook each serving separately, but if you have to double up, don't crowd the meat in the pan. Serve with bread to sop up the juices in the pan.

2 strip or top sirloin steaks (6 ounces each) completely trimmed of any fat or sinew

1½ teaspoons kosher salt

1 Tablespoon coarsely cracked black pepper

¼ cup extra-virgin olive oil

4 teaspoons chopped fresh rosemary

3 ounces arugula (about 3½ cups, loosely packed), tough stems removed, leaves very well washed and dried

½ lemon, cut in wedges

Season the beef with a little bit of the salt and pepper. Sear the steaks briefly on a hot grill or in a heavy pan to brown the outside. Remove from the grill (the center will still be raw). When cool enough to handle, slice the steaks on an angle into ½-inch slices. Fan them so they're almost flat on individual heatproof pans or plates (see note above). Drizzle with the olive oil and sprinkle on the rosemary and the rest of the salt and pepper.

Put the pans on a grill or on a burner and heat until the oil begins to bubble and the meat is cooked to rare, about 5 minutes. Carefully remove from the heat and surround each steak with the arugula. Squeeze the lemon on the arugula (if you put the juice on the meat, it will turn the beef gray). Serve immediately.

—TONY MANTUANO

COOKING AHEAD

Whole beef fillet works well as part of a buffet because it tastes just as good at room temperature as it does hot.

Roasted Filet of Beef with Whole-Grain Mustard & Herb Crust

SERVES 10

This is a perfect—and perfectly easy—dish to make for a crowd. If you have a heavy-duty roasting pan, sear the filets right in the pan on the stove. Otherwise, use a large, heavy-based skillet.

¼ cup whole-grain mustard
3 Tablespoons extra-virgin olive oil
1 Tablespoon dried savory, finely crumbled
1 Tablespoon dried thyme, finely crumbled
1 whole filet of beef (7 to 8 pounds untrimmed or 5 to 6 pounds trimmed)
  Vegetable oil for sautéing
  Coarse salt and freshly ground black pepper

In a small bowl, mix together the mustard, olive oil, savory, and thyme.

Trim the meat of all excess fat and silverskin. Cut the filet in half to make two equal pieces about 7 inches long. You'll have one piece with the broad double-pieced butt portion and a thinner piece that tapers to a small tip. Tuck the tapered tip under and tie with twine to fashion two equally thick roasts. Tie each roast at 2-inch intervals.

Heat the oven to 450°F. Heat a heavy-duty roasting pan or large skillet over medium-high heat. Pour in enough vegetable oil to just cover the bottom of the pan. Pat the filets dry, salt them generously, and lay them in the pan; cook without disturbing them until the bottoms are a rich brown. Turn the beef and sear the other sides, for about 4 minutes each to get a good sear. Transfer the fillets to a cutting board, brush them with the mustard and herb mix, and then generously grind fresh pepper over them.

Put a rack in the roasting pan, lay the meat on the rack, and roast until the internal temperature reaches 125°F to 130°F for medium rare, about 25 minutes. (Check after 15 minutes; roasting time will vary depending on searing time.) Remove the filets from the oven and let them rest in a warm spot for at least 15 minutes before slicing.

COOKING RIGHT

Be generous with the mustard-herb mixture, and it will give the mild tasting meat a big hit of wonderful flavor.

—KATHERINE ALFORD

COOKING RIGHT

After you add the wine, use a wooden spoon or spatula to scrape up the flavorful bits stuck to the bottom of the pan. Then reduce the liquid to intensify the flavor of the sauce.

Filet of Beef with Blue Cheese, Rosemary & Pine Nut Sauce

SERVES 2

This recipe gives you the chance to use up some hearty red wine:
The beef and blue cheese help to soften the tannins in those kinds of reds.

1   Tablespoon vegetable oil
2   sliced filet mignon (5 to 6 ounces each), lightly pounded to about
    ¾ inch thick, seasoned with salt and freshly ground black pepper
1   Tablespoon unsalted butter
2   shallots, minced
¾   cup full-bodied red wine, such as Cabernet Sauvignon
¾   cup homemade or low-salt canned chicken stock
1   Tablespoon fresh rosemary, chopped
2   Tablespoons crumbled blue cheese
2   Tablespoons pine nuts, toasted in a dry skillet and chopped

In a medium, nonreactive skillet, heat the oil over high heat. When the oil is hot, sear the meat on both sides until well browned, about 3 minutes per side for medium rare. Transfer the meat to a platter and tent it with foil to keep warm. Pour the excess oil out of the pan, making sure to hold back the cooked-on juices and browned bits. Reduce the heat to medium high and add the butter. When the butter is melted, add the shallots, sautéing until softened, about 1 minute. Add the wine and cook at a vigorous simmer, scraping up the browned bits with a wooden spoon and reducing until the liquid is very syrupy. Add the stock and rosemary; continue boiling until the liquid is reduced by half. Remove from the heat. Stir in the blue cheese, along with any juices that have run off the meat; the cheese should melt just slightly. Spoon the sauce over the meat, garnish with the chopped pine nuts, and serve.

—BRIAN STREETER

Beef Kebabs with Soy Sauce, Cumin & Orange Zest

SERVES 4

These kebabs would also be delicious made with lamb.
Serve with grilled zucchini and eggplant and some rice.

1 Tablespoon brown sugar

¼ cup soy sauce

1 large clove garlic, very finely chopped

1½ teaspoons ground cumin

¾ teaspoon ground coriander

   Pinch cayenne

¼ teaspoon freshly ground black pepper

1 Tablespoon fresh lemon juice

¾ teaspoon grated orange zest

2 Tablespoons olive oil

1¾ pounds boneless rib-eye steak, about 1½ to 2 inches thick
   and cut into 1½- to 2-inch cubes

   Sprigs of fresh cilantro or mint

   Plain yogurt (optional)

In a large bowl, combine the brown sugar and soy sauce. Whisk in the garlic, spices, lemon juice, and orange zest, and gradually whisk in the olive oil.

Set aside 2 tablespoons of the marinade. Toss the beef cubes in the bowl with the rest of the marinade and marinate for 30 minutes at room temperature or for up to 8 hours in the refrigerator.

Prepare a medium-hot charcoal fire or heat a gas grill. Skewer the cubes, leaving a little space between each cube so they'll cook all around. Grill, turning the skewers to brown on all sides to the point of slight charring, for about 8 minutes for medium rare.

Push the meat off the skewers and onto plates, drizzle with the reserved 2 tablespoons marinade, and garnish with cilantro or mint sprigs and a spoonful of yogurt, if you like.

—LESLIE REVSIN

COOKING RIGHT

For a more pronounced cumin flavor, grind whole cumin seeds with a mortar and pestle or in a coffee grinder devoted to spices.

Grilled Flank Steak with Habanero Mojo

SERVES 4 TO 6

COOKING RIGHT

A classic mojo starts with a mortar and pestle, but you can also use a food processor.

Toss a few red onions on the grill to serve with this dish; a salad of tomatoes and cucumbers rounds out the meal nicely. This versatile mojo works well on chicken and shrimp, too.

For the *mojo*:

12 cloves garlic (or 4 Tablespoons minced garlic)
 2 habaneros or other spicy chiles, cored, seeded, and minced (wear rubber gloves)
 1 teaspoon kosher salt
 4 teaspoons whole cumin seeds, toasted
 1 cup olive oil
 ⅔ cup sour orange juice (or ⅓ cup fresh lime juice plus ⅓ cup fresh orange juice)
1½ Tablespoons sherry vinegar
    Salt and freshly ground black pepper

For the steak:

1½ pounds flank steak
 1 or 2 large Bermuda onions, thickly sliced and brushed with olive oil (optional)
    Salt and freshly ground black pepper

Make the mojo—Mash the raw garlic, chiles, salt, and cumin together in a mortar and pestle until fairly smooth. (Alternatively, use a food processor, pulsing until the ingredients are finely chopped but not puréed.) Scrape the mixture into a bowl and set aside.

JUST WHAT IS A MOJO?

A mojo (pronounced MOE-HOE) is not really one sauce, but a family of tropically inspired sauces. Bursting with bold flavors such as garlic, chiles, fruit juices, and fresh herbs, this warm vinaigrette made its way to the New World from Spain and is hugely popular in the Caribbean. Miami chef Norman Van Aiken has helped popularize the sauce here, and you can now find mojos on menus in every part of the country.

Heat the olive oil until fairly hot but not smoking, and pour it over the garlic-chile mixture (the oil will sizzle), stir, and let stand 10 minutes to cook the garlic slightly. Whisk in the sour orange juice and vinegar. Season with salt and pepper and cool completely.

Put the steak in a zip-top bag or a shallow bowl and pour in 1 cup of the cooled mojo. Seal and refrigerate for at least 2 hours or overnight, turning occasionally. Refrigerate the remaining 1 cup of mojo.

Cook and serve—Light a charcoal or gas grill. When the grill is very hot, remove the steak from the marinade (discard the marinade), pat dry, and season with salt and pepper; cook 5 to 7 minutes on one side and 3 to 4 minutes on the other for medium rare. Remove from the grill and let rest for 5 minutes. (If you like, grill the Bermuda onions as well—you can put them on at the same time as the flank steak; grill 6 to 7 minutes per side.) Meanwhile, warm the reserved mojo over low heat. Slice the flank steak very thinly on the bias and serve with the reserved mojo and the grilled onions.

—NORMAN VAN AKEN

COOKING RIGHT

Hot oil takes the edge off the garlic and heats up the spices, intensifying their flavor.

COOKING RIGHT

Slice "across the grain," or perpendicular to the long muscle fibers that run parallel to one another. That way, the fibers become shorter, making the meat more tender and easier to chew.

Garlicky Beef over Lettuce Greens
SERVES 4

Inspired by Asian dishes where the meat is used more as an accent than the focus, this dish is full flavored yet wonderfully light, perfect for a light summer dinner.

1 pound lean beef (like top round or flank steak), trimmed and thinly sliced across the grain into strips 1 inch wide and 2 to 3 inches long
1 Tablespoon fish sauce
5 Tablespoons extra-virgin olive oil
    kosher salt and freshly ground black pepper
¼ teaspoon sugar
¼ teaspoon crushed red chile flakes
1 small onion, thinly sliced
5 large cloves garlic, coarsely chopped
2 Tablespoons apple-cider vinegar
1 teaspoon Dijon mustard
1 large ripe tomato, cored and cut into chunks
1 head romaine lettuce, washed, drained, and torn into bite-size pieces

In a medium bowl, combine the beef with the fish sauce, 1 tablespoon of the olive oil, ¼ teaspoon salt, ½ teaspoon pepper, the sugar, and the chile flakes. Heat a large skillet or frying pan over medium-high heat. Add 2 tablespoon of the olive oil. When the oil is very hot, add the onions and garlic and cook, stirring, until they're slightly golden, about 2 minutes. Add the beef and cook, tossing and stirring briskly, until it reaches medium rare, about 1 minute. Remove from the heat.

In a small bowl, whisk together the vinegar and mustard. Add the remaining 2 tablespoons oil in a slow stream, whisking constantly. Season with ¾ teaspoon salt and ¼ teaspoon pepper. Drizzle the beef with 2 tablespoons of the vinaigrette and toss to combine. Toss the lettuce with the remaining vinaigrette and garnish with the tomato. Lay the beef, onions, and garlic on top of the salad and serve immediately.

—FINE COOKING STAFF

COOKING RIGHT

Salting the meat overnight tenderizes the ribs and gives it a more concentrated flavor.

Beef Short Ribs Braised in Red Wine
SERVES 8

For the best results, you'll want to salt the ribs for at least 8 hours before cooking them. Serve these meltingly tender ribs with polenta (see p. 77) and sautéed Swiss chard (see p. 174).

 8 lean bone-in short ribs (about 8 pounds total)
 1 teaspoon kosher salt
    Freshly ground black pepper
 1 large carrot, diced
 1 rib celery, diced
 1 large onion, diced
 ¼ cup chopped fresh parsley
 2 cups red wine
1¼ cups water

The night before you cook the ribs, trim any excess fat and sprinkle each rib on all sides with a scant teaspoon salt. Set a cooling rack on a baking sheet and put the ribs on the rack. Cover with plastic wrap and refrigerate at least 8 hours.

Heat the oven to 350°F. Season the ribs with pepper. In a heavy frying pan over medium-high heat, brown the ribs well on all sides in batches. Pour off all but 2 tablespoons of the fat. Add the carrot, celery, and onion. Reduce the heat and cook, scraping up the browned bits on the bottom of the pan, until the vegetables begin to soften, about 5 minutes.

Spread the vegetables on the bottom of a sided baking pan that will accommodate the ribs. Set the ribs on top of the vegetables and add the parsley, wine, and water. Cover the pan tightly with aluminum foil and cook in the hot oven until the ribs are very tender but not falling off the bone, about 2½ hours.

Pour the braising liquid through a strainer into a saucepan and spoon off all visible fat. Gently boil until reduced by about one third.

Serve the ribs on warm plates and sauce them generously with the reduced cooking liquid.

—PAUL BERTOLLI

COOK'S CHOICE

Choose the meatiest short ribs you can find. If possible, have your butcher cut them to include three bones as the ones here do.

Fragrant Beef Short Ribs with Ginger, Star Anise & Leeks

SERVES 6

The soy sauce seasons the ribs well (no need to salt them before searing) and produces an intense sauce that's delicious with mashed potatoes.

1⅓ cups drained canned whole tomatoes, coarsely chopped

½ cup soy sauce

½ cup fino sherry, dry white wine, or dry vermouth

2 Tablespoons light brown sugar

4 whole star anise

6 to 6½ pounds beef short ribs on the bone (each 3 to 4 inches long)
   Freshly ground black pepper

1½ Tablespoons vegetable oil; more as needed

6 cloves garlic, smashed and peeled

1 piece fresh ginger (about 1 inch), peeled and cut into 8 slices

6 large scallions (white and green parts), cut into 2-inch lengths

1 Tablespoon unsalted butter

3 medium leeks (white and light green parts), cut into 2-inch-long julienne strips (2 to 2½ cups), rinsed, and dried well
   Kosher salt

Position a rack in the center of the oven and heat the oven to 325°F. Put the tomatoes, ⅔ cup water, the soy sauce, sherry, and brown sugar in a bowl and stir. Add the star anise.

Pat the short ribs dry with paper towels and season them with pepper. In an ovenproof pot that's large enough to hold all the ribs in no more than two layers, heat the oil over medium-high heat. Put as many ribs in the pot as will fit without crowding and brown them on all sides, about 2 minutes per side. Transfer to a platter. Brown the rest of the ribs, adding more oil if needed, and transfer to the platter.

Pour off the fat from the pan, reduce the heat to low, and add the garlic, ginger, and scallions, stirring and pressing them against the pot, for 1 to 2 minutes to bring out their flavor. Return the ribs to the pot and pour the tomato and soy sauce mixture over them. Bring to a simmer and cover. Transfer the pot to the oven and braise the ribs, lifting and turning

COOKING RIGHT

Sweet, buttery leeks are such a perfect accompaniment to the full flavored beef that they're included right in the recipe. Some mashed potatoes would round out the plate.

them about every half hour, until the meat is very tender and starts to fall off the bone when pulled with a fork, 2½ to 3 hours.

Transfer the ribs to a serving platter (or if you're working ahead, transfer them to a baking dish; refrigerate, them to a baking dish; refrigerate, covered, when cool). Pick out and discard the ginger and star anise from the pot and pour the remaining sauce into a large, clear measuring cup. When the fat rises to the surface, after about 5 minutes, spoon it off and discard. (Or, if you're working ahead, cool the sauce in the pot, refrigerate it, and skim the solid fat off the top. When it's time to reheat the ribs, return them to the pot and heat gently in the oven.)

Meanwhile, melt the butter in a large skillet over medium-high heat. Add the leeks and cook, stirring frequently, until they begin to brown, 3 to 5 minutes. Reduce the heat to medium low and continue cooking, stirring frequently, until tender, about 3 to 5 minutes. Season with salt and pepper.

Reheat the sauce, season generously with pepper and more salt, if you like, and pour it over the ribs. Scatter the leeks over the top and serve.

—LESLIE REVSIN

COOKING AHEAD

Cooking and cooling the braised ribs at least a day before serving helps the flavors marry and makes degreasing easy.

BEAUTIFUL, AROMATIC ANISE

Star anise is a whole star-shaped spice that's wonderfully reminiscent of licorice, clove, fennel seed, and aniseed. It's used often in Chinese and Vietnamese cooking to infuse soups, stews, and braised dishes (much like bay leaves are used in Western cooking). Some supermarkets carry whole star anise, but you'll definitely find it at an Asian market, or try a mail-order spice source.

Quick Stovetop-Braised Sirloin Tips with Mushroom Sauce

SERVES 4

Sirloin tips are a great choice for a quick braise, as they're full of flavor and will have a pleasantly chewy texture after 20 minutes of cooking (further cooking would toughen them). Buttered noodles or mashed potatoes would make a good accompaniment for this quickly prepared dish.

COOKING RIGHT

Look for this dark brown color when searing the steaks. A good sear intensifies the meat's flavor as well as the flavor of the sauce.

1	teaspoon dry mustard
1	teaspoon light brown sugar
½	teaspoon dried thyme leaves, crushed
½	teaspoon ground ginger
½	teaspoon sweet paprika
	Kosher salt
1½	pounds sirloin tip steaks, ¾ to 1 inch thick
½	pound fresh mushrooms, preferably a mix of half shiitakes and half cremini
2	Tablespoons olive oil or vegetable oil
2	Tablespoons unsalted butter
4	scallions, thinly sliced, white and light green parts separated from dark green parts (save both)
1	cup dark ale or porter beer (such as Beck's Dark)
2	teaspoons Worcestershire sauce

Mix the mustard, brown sugar, thyme, ginger, paprika, and 1 teaspoon salt in a small bowl until well combined. Coat both sides of the steaks with the spice mix.

Remove and discard the stems from the shiitakes, if using, and trim the stem ends from the cremini. Wipe all the mushrooms clean and slice them ¼ inch thick.

Heat the oil in a large skillet over medium-high heat. When the oil is shimmering, add half the steaks and sear them until nicely browned, 2 to 3 minutes per side (the steaks will brown quickly because of the sugar in the spice mix). Transfer to a plate and repeat with the remaining steaks.

Reduce the heat to medium, add 1 tablespoon of the butter to the
pan, and let it melt. Add the mushrooms, the scallion whites, and
¼ teaspoon salt and cook, stirring occasionally with a wooden spoon,
until the mushrooms soften and brown, 4 to 6 minutes. Pour in the beer
and Worcestershire. Scrape the bottom of the pan with a spoon, raise
the heat to medium high, bring to a boil, and cook, uncovered, until the
liquid is reduced by half, about 4 minutes. Return the steaks and any
accumulated juices to the pan, cover tightly with a lid or foil, and reduce
the heat to a low simmer. Braise, turning the steaks after 8 minutes,
until tender and just cooked through (they should be easy to slice with
a paring knife), about 16 minutes total. Transfer the steaks to a cutting
board and slice them thinly. Cut the remaining 1 tablespoon butter
into four pieces and swirl them into the sauce. Stir in the scallion greens
and taste for seasoning. Serve the steak slices topped with the sauce.

—MOLLY STEVENS

Pork Roast with Fennel & Pears

SERVES 4 TO 6

The fennel and pears soften during cooking but keep their shape so you can serve them alongside the slices of pork.

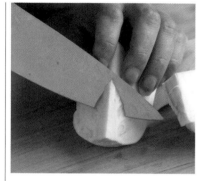

COOKING RIGHT

Before chopping the fennel bulb, discard any tough outer leaves, cut it into quarters, and slice away its tough core as shown above.

3- to 4-pound pork butt, well trimmed
4 cloves garlic, slivered
1 bulb fennel, trimmed, cored, and very coarsely chopped (about 1½ cups)
3 shallots, minced
3 ripe pears, peeled, cored, and cut into a large dice
¼ cup dry sherry
¼ cup homemade or low-salt canned chicken stock
1 Tablespoon fennel seeds, chopped
1½ teaspoons salt
¾ teaspoon freshly ground black pepper

Heat the oven to 350°F. Poke the meat all over with a thin-bladed knife and insert the garlic slivers into the holes. Put the fennel, shallots, pears, sherry, and stock into a large casserole or small roasting pan; toss to combine. Put the pork in the pan and pat the fennel seeds over the pork. Sprinkle the pork with the salt and pepper. Cover the pan with a lid or foil, and cook the pork until it's easily pierced with a fork and its juices run clear, 3½ to 4 hours. Remove the roast from the oven and allow it to rest in the pan for 5 to 10 minutes before carving. Slice and serve with the fennel, pears, and pan juices (degreased if necessary) spooned over the top.

—LUCIA WATSON AND BETH DOOLEY

Grilled Pork Rib Chops with Fresh Herb Rub

SERVES 4

This fragrant rub not only adds flavor, but it also protects the surface of the meat, keeping it from drying out during grilling. Serve the chops with the chickpea salad on p. 156 or the Lemon Rice Salad on p. 157.

1 Tablespoon chopped garlic
1 Tablespoon crushed fennel seeds
1 Tablespoon finely chopped fresh sage
1 Tablespoon finely chopped fresh rosemary
2 teaspoons coarse salt
2 teaspoons coarsely ground black pepper
4 bone-in pork rib chops, ¾ to 1 inch thick (2½ to 3 pounds total), brined if you like (see Cooking Right on p. 120)

In a small food processor, combine the garlic, fennel seeds, sage, rosemary, salt, and pepper. Pulse several times to blend well. Lightly coat each chop on both sides with the herb rub.

Build and light a charcoal fire so there are thicker and thinner layers of coals for areas of varying heat. For a gas grill, set one side to medium high and the other side to low.

When the thicker area of coals is medium hot (you'll be able to hold your hand just above the grate for about 2 seconds), set the chops directly over them, or over the medium-high area on a gas grill. If flare-ups occur, move the chops momentarily to a cooler area. Sear the chops over the hotter area for about 1½ minutes per side and then use tongs to move them to the area that's less hot. Cover the grill and continue cooking until the chops are firm and their internal temperature reaches 145° to 150°F, another 3 to 4 minutes per side.

Transfer the chops to a clean platter and let them rest for 5 minutes so the juices redistribute and the chops finish cooking.

—BRUCE AIDELLS

COOKING RIGHT

Practice using touch to gauge doneness. An instant-read thermometer will read 145°F to 150°F, and the chops will just have begun to feel firm to the touch when it's time to pull them off the heat.

Glazed & Grilled Pork Tenderloin

SERVES 4 TO 5

This master grilling recipe works perfectly, no matter how you flavor the pork. Choose one of the glazes on the facing page for a beautiful crust, or use your own favorite marinade or dry rub (just keep it low in salt if you brine the pork).

2 pork tenderloins (about 2 pounds total), trimmed and brined, if you like, as described at left

1 recipe concentrated fruit glaze of your choice (see the recipes on the facing page) Freshly ground black pepper

Rub the brined tenderloins all over with the glaze and then season with the pepper. Or, season to taste with another flavoring of your choice.

Heat a gas grill, turning all the burners to high until the grill is fully heated, 10 to 15 minutes.

Put the pork on the hot grill grate. Close the lid and grill for 7 minutes. Turn the pork over, close the lid, and grill for another 6 minutes. Turn off the heat (keep the lid closed) and continue to cook the pork until its temperature at its thickest reads 145° to 150°F, another 5 minutes. Remove the pork from the grill and let it rest for 5 minutes before carving. Cut across the grain into ½-inch slices and serve immediately.

Note to charcoal grill users: Your timing might vary depending on how hot and how consistent your fire is. To use a charcoal grill, prepare a two-zone fire, banking all the coals to one side of the grill. Position the tenderloins directly over the hot coals, cook (covered) until nicely seared on both sides, turning only once, and then move them to the coolest part of the grill (over no coals), again with the lid closed, for the last 5 minutes.

—PAM ANDERSON

COOKING RIGHT

You don't have to brine the pork before glazing and grilling, but it will be even more tender and flavorful if you do. Here's how: Mix ½ cup kosher salt and ½ cup sugar with 1 quart cool water until dissolved. Submerge the trimmed tenderloins in the brine and let stand about 45 minutes. Remove, rinse, and pat dry.

GLAZES & SAUCES ADD FLAVOR

Sweet Chile Glaze

YIELDS ENOUGH TO GLAZE 2 PORK TENDERLOINS

- 2 teaspoons vegetable oil
- 2 teaspoons chile powder
- ½ teaspoon ground cumin
- ¼ cup frozen pineapple juice concentrate, thawed

In a small saucepan, heat the oil, chile powder, and cumin over medium heat. When the mixture starts to sizzle and the spices are fragrant, add the concentrate. Simmer until the mixture reduces to about 2 tablespoons. Set aside to cool slightly.

Sage-Orange Glaze

YIELDS ENOUGH TO GLAZE 2 PORK TENDERLOINS

- ¼ cup frozen orange juice concentrate, thawed
- 1 teaspoon brown sugar
- 2 teaspoons dried rubbed sage

In a small saucepan, bring the concentrate, brown sugar, and sage to a simmer. Simmer until the mixture reduces to about 2 tablespoons. Set aside to cool slightly.

Curry-Apple Glaze

YIELDS ENOUGH TO GLAZE 2 PORK TENDERLOINS

- 2 teaspoons vegetable oil
- 1 Tablespoon curry powder
- ¼ cup frozen apple juice concentrate, thawed

In a small saucepan over medium heat, heat the oil and curry powder. When the mixture starts to sizzle and the curry is fragrant, add the concentrate. Simmer until the mixture reduces to about 3 tablespoons. Set aside to cool slightly.

Mango Chutney Sauce

YIELDS ABOUT ⅓ CUP

- ⅓ cup Major Grey's mango chutney
- 4 teaspoons rice vinegar
  Freshly ground black pepper
- 1 teaspoon minced fresh cilantro (optional)

Combine all the ingredients. Pass the sauce separately when serving the pork tenderloins. ◆

To keep lean pork moist, use a moderately hot oven and a covered pot. Don't overcook it! Older guidelines suggest cooking to as high as 170°F, but a tastier temperature is 145°F, which is considered safe by the FDA.

Pot-Roasted Pork Loin
Stuffed with Prunes & Dried Apricots

SERVES 4 TO 6

In this recipe, the pork loin is stuffed with fruit and almonds and served in a spicy red wine sauce that's reminiscent of sauerbraten. Use a full-bodied red wine, such as one from the Rhône or a Syrah. Wild rice and glazed carrots are good accompaniments.

1   boneless pork loin (2 pounds)

½   cup dried apricots

4   to 6 whole blanched almonds, toasted in a dry skillet

½   cup pitted prunes
    Kosher salt and freshly ground black pepper

2   Tablespoons unsalted butter

1   Tablespoon vegetable oil

1   onion, chopped

2   teaspoons chopped fresh thyme

½   teaspoon ground cinnamon

¼   teaspoon ground cloves

¼   teaspoon ground nutmeg

¼   cup red-wine vinegar

2   cups dry red wine

1   cup veal stock or homemade or low-salt canned chicken broth; more if needed

Heat the oven to 350°F. Trim the pork and butterfly it (see the left photo on the facing page). Stuff 4 to 6 of the apricots with almonds and wrap each apricot with a prune. Lay the prunes along the center of the cut surface of the pork, adding more stuffed fruit if needed. Roll and tie the roast (see photo on right on the facing page). Sprinkle it on all sides with salt and pepper. Coarsely chop the remaining prunes and apricots.

Heat the butter and oil in a Dutch oven or other large, heavy-based pot over medium-high heat and brown the pork thoroughly on all sides, 8 to 10 minutes total. Take out the pork, add the onion, and sauté until it starts to turn brown, about 3 minutes. Stir in ½ teaspoon pepper, the

thyme, cinnamon, cloves, and nutmeg and cook, stirring, until fragrant, 1 minute. Add the vinegar and simmer 1 minute. Add the wine and simmer until it's reduced by almost half, 10 to 12 minutes. Stir in the chopped fruit and the stock or broth. Add the pork, pushing it down into the sauce, cover the pot, and bring to a boil.

Put the pork in the heated oven and cook, basting with the pan juices and turning occasionally, until an instant-read thermometer inserted in the center of the meat registers 145°F, about 45 minutes. If the sauce reduces rapidly during cooking, add more broth. When the pork is done, the sauce should be dark and reduced by about half with a slightly thick consistency; if it's thin, remove the meat and reduce the sauce by simmering it on the stovetop. Let the meat rest for about 10 minutes before carving it into thick slices. Serve with some sauce spooned over it.

—ANNE WILLAN

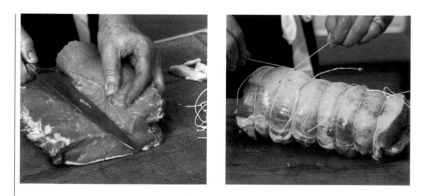

BUTTERFLYING AND TYING A BONELESS PORK LOIN

To butterfly the loin: Use a sharp knife to cut a large slit in the loin, cutting almost through to the other side. Open the meat flat, like a book, so it's an even thickness.

To tie the loin: You can use the more advanced butcher's knot if you know how or just tie individual strings as the photo above right shows. Either way, pull snugly but not too tightly and keep the intervals between the knots even for a roast that looks good, cooks evenly, and carves easily.

COOKING RIGHT

For easiest slicing: Put the cooked ribs on the cutting board meaty-side down.

Chinese-Style Spareribs

SERVES 4 TO 6 AS A MAIN COURSE

These ribs taste great with the quick and easy dipping sauce shown here (see recipe at left).

- 2 Tablespoons ground coriander
- 2 Tablespoons hot chile powder
- 2 Tablespoons dark brown sugar
- 1 Tablespoon five-spice powder
- 1 Tablespoon ground fennel seeds
- 1 Tablespoon kosher salt, plus more for sprinkling
- 1 teaspoon dried red chile flakes
- 2 full (13-rib) racks of St. Louis-cut pork spareribs (about 3 pounds each)

In a small bowl, stir together all the ingredients except the ribs.

Position a rack in the center of the oven and heat the oven to 300°F.

Sprinkle and press the rub on both sides of each rib rack. Put the racks, meaty side up, on a broiling pan or a wire roasting rack set over a baking sheet. Lightly season the ribs with salt and put them in the oven. After the first hour, rotate the pan every 30 minutes. The ribs will sizzle gently as they cook, and they'll become tender after about 2 hours in the oven.

To test for doneness, pick up the center of the ribs with tongs; the ends of the ribs should flop downward (this means the fat and cartilage have broken down), and a skewer inserted between the ribs should meet little resistance. If the meat between the ribs is still tough, keep cooking, checking every 15 minutes and rotating the pan.

Remove the rib racks from the oven, put them on a cutting board meaty side down, slice them into individual ribs, and serve.

—STEVE JOHNSON

Dipping Sauce

- ¼ cup soy sauce
- 2 Tablespoons sugar
- 2 Tablespoons rice vinegar
- 1 Tablespoon minced fresh ginger
- 1 teaspoon sesame oil

Add all ingredients to a pot and bring to a simmer. Cool to room temperature and serve on the side.

Grilled Sausage & Onion Panini

SERVES 4 AS A MAIN COURSE

In this recipe, grillng the bread on a regular gas grill substitutes for pressing the bread in an actual panini grill. Both give the bread a toasty flavor and grill marks. Of course, if you have a panini maker, you can use that to finish the sandwich.

1   large red onion, sliced crosswise into ¼-inch disks

5   Tablespoons olive oil

1   Tablespoon plus 1 teaspoon good balsamic vinegar
     Kosher salt and freshly ground black pepper

1   large ripe tomato (about 8 ounces), thinly sliced

8   slices (about ½ inch thick each) crusty Italian bread

1   clove garlic, smashed

4   links sweet or hot Italian sausage (about 1 pound total)

1   packed cup arugula, washed (if the leaves are large, stem them)

2   to 3 Tablespoons freshly grated Parmigiano Reggiano

COOK'S CHOICE

If you're hankering for the flavors of a classic sausage and pepper grinder, leave off the tomato and arugula and add grilled red pepper to the sandwich.

Heat a gas grill to high. Drizzle the onions with 1 tablespoon oil and 1 tablespoon vinegar and season well with salt and pepper. Toss gently to keep the disks intact. Season the tomato with salt and pepper and drizzle with 1 tablespoon oil. Brush 2 tablespoons of the oil over both sides of the bread, rub with the smashed garlic, and season with salt and pepper.

Put the sausages and onions on the hottest part of the grill. Grill the onions, turning them a few times, until they're browned and soft, about 8 minutes. Grill the sausages, turning occasionally, until fully cooked, 10 to 12 minutes. Grill the bread for 1 to 2 minutes on each side.

Dress the arugula with the remaining 1 tablespoon oil and 1 teaspoon vinegar; season with salt and pep-per. Divide the arugula and tomato slices among four of the bread slices. Slice the sausages in half lengthwise and lay them over the tomatoes. Lay the grilled onion and the Parmigiano over the sausages. Top with the remaining bread. Slice the sandwiches in half and serve.

—TONY ROSENFELD

Sweet & Spicy Broiled Ham Steak

SERVES 2

Transform a humble slice of ham into a sophisitcated weeknight dish with a glaze that's got it all: sweet marmalade, hot pepper flakes, tangy vinegar, and fragrant rosemary.

¾ to 1 pound ham steak, ½ to ¾ inch thick
⅓ cup orange marmalade
1 Tablespoon cider vinegar
1½ teaspoons chopped fresh rosemary
½ teaspoon dry mustard
½ teaspoon soy sauce
　Pinch crushed red chile flakes

Arrange an oven rack so a broiler pan will be able to sit 2 to 3 inches away from the element and heat the broiler on high (or prepare a hot charcoal or gas grill fire).

Pat the ham steak dry with paper towels and set on the broiler pan (or on a plate for transferring to the grill). In a small saucepan, combine the marmalade, vinegar, rosemary, mustard, soy sauce, and chile flakes. Bring to a simmer over medium heat and cook, whisking to combine, for 2 to 3 minutes. Keep warm. Brush one side of the ham with the glaze and broil (or grill) until the glaze is bubbling and browned, 4 to 5 minutes. Flip, brush on the remaining glaze, and cook the other side for another 4 to 5 minutes. Serve immediately.

—MOLLY STEVENS

COOK'S CHOICE

If you don't have rosemary, try another herb: thyme, basil, mint, and cilantro would work in the glaze, each providing its own unique herbal note.

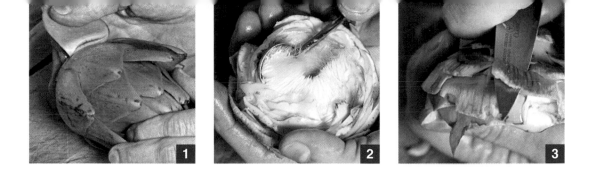

Braised Lamb Chops with Artichokes

SERVES 2 GENEROUSLY

Fresh artichokes taste great with lamb, but frozen hearts will do in a pinch: thaw them, pat them dry, and add them about half an hour after you've added the olives.

4 lamb shoulder blade or arm chops, ¾ inch thick
  Salt and freshly ground black pepper
2 Tablespoons olive oil
2 cloves garlic, minced
2 teaspoons chopped fresh rosemary
2 teaspoons tomato paste
1 cup homemade or low-salt canned beef broth
½ cup dry white wine
  Juice of 1 lemon (for artichokes)
2 large artichokes
¼ cup niçoise or other good-quality black olives, pitted

Heat a heavy, straight-sided skillet over medium-high heat. Season both sides of the chops with salt and pepper. Add the olive oil to the pan and sear the chops on both sides until well browned, about 3 minutes per side. Sprinkle the garlic and rosemary over the chops in the pan. Whisk the tomato paste into the beef broth and pour it over the lamb; add the wine. Bring to a boil, reduce the heat to a slow simmer, cover, and simmer for 30 minutes.

Meanwhile, prepare the artichokes as directed above.

After the lamb has simmered for 30 minutes, remove the artichokes from the water and stuff them between the chops in the pan. Sprinkle the olives over the chops. Continue simmering, covered, until the chops are very tender and the artichokes are cooked through, 40 to 45 minutes. Put two chops on each plate and spoon the artichokes, olives, and pan juices over them.

—BRIAN STREETER

PREPARING ARTICHOKES

1 Trim the stem flush with the bottom and snap off the dark outer green leaves.

2 Cut the top third of the artichoke and with a spoon scoop out and discard the hairy choke and purple inner leaves.

3 With a paring knife, trim the outside and bottom to reveal a tender yellow and pale green layer. Cut the artichoke in half lengthwise and then cut each half into 4 wedges. Reserve the artichokes in water combined with lemon juice.

Spice-Crusted Lamb Chops with Cilantro-Yogurt Sauce

SERVES 4

For this recipe, be sure to use whole spices and crush them yourself. Preground spices are too fine to form a crust, and they'll turn bitter during cooking. For a brightly flavored side dish, serve the lamb chop with the black bean, mango, and jicama salad on p. 154, or go with the rosemary-scented white beans on p. 152.

For the spice rub and lamb:

1 Tablespoon coriander seeds
1 Tablespoon cumin seeds
1 Tablespoon fennel seeds
1 teaspoon kosher salt
¼ teaspoon freshly ground white pepper
2 to 2½ pounds loin or rib chops
  (about 4 chops, 1½ inches thick)
2 Tablespoons oil

For the sauce:

6 Tablespoons plain yogurt (not low- or nonfat)
½ teaspoon coriander seeds
2 cloves garlic, finely minced
  Freshly ground white pepper
1 teaspoon honey
3 Tablespoons fresh lime juice
4 Tablespoons extra-virgin olive oil
1 cup loosely packed fresh cilantro leaves, finely chopped
  Kosher salt

Make the spice rub—Crush the coriander, cumin, and fennel seeds in a mortar and pestle or by pulsing in a coffee grinder dedicated to spices. Combine with the salt and pepper. The mixture should have a sandy texture; don't turn it into a powder.

COOKING RIGHT

To chop tender herbs, choke up with one hand on a large, sharp chef's knife. Use the other hand to anchor the tip of the knife, allowing you to pivot the blade over the leaves while moving the handle up and down. After a little chopping, gather the leaves back into a pile with the side of the knife and continue chopping.

Make the sauce—Put the yogurt in a very fine strainer or a coffee filter and suspend it over a bowl. Let it stand for 20 minutes. Crush the coriander seeds and combine them with the garlic, pepper, honey, and lime juice. Beat in the olive oil and then mix in the yogurt until just incorporated. Fold in the cilantro. Season with salt and pepper. This sauce can be prepared up to a day in advance and stored, tightly covered, in the refrigerator.

Cook the chops—A few minutes before cooking the chops, unwrap them and pat them dry. Press the spices onto the chops, coating the surface thoroughly; this will become the crust. Heat a heavy skillet over medium heat until very hot. Add the oil, immediately followed by the chops. If the pan is not large enough to hold all the chops, cook them in batches. If you crowd them in the pan, the crust won't form as well. Cook the chops about 9 minutes per side per inch of meat for medium rare (about 13 minutes per side in this case). Serve with the sauce.

—JOSH EISEN

CHOOSING THE RIGHT CHOP

Rib chops are delicate and tender. These chops are the ones you find on a rack of lamb. You may find the chops frenched, meaning the ends of the bone are scraped of all meat, fat, and connective tissue, but you'll actually get more flavor if most of that is left on as pictured top left.

Loin chops are compact and meaty. These come from the very tender lamb loin and are often cut into thick chops. Like rib chops, these are tender enough to be sautéed.

Shoulder chops are tasty but bony. Less expensive than loin or rib chops, these come from the shoulder. Though they have several bones running through them, they are very tasty and a good value, especially if you plan to braise them.

Lamb Brochettes with Black Olive & Mint Vinaigrette

SERVES 8; YIELDS 2 CUPS VINAIGRETTE

The intense meaty flavor of these brochettes is nicely offset by a vibrantly flavored vinaigrette.

For the olive and mint vinaigrette:

2 cloves garlic
1 Tablespoon capers, rinsed
3 ounces (½ cup) kalamata or other good-quality black olives, pitted
3 shallots, thinly sliced
1 Tablespoon grainy mustard
1 Tablespoon chopped fresh marjoram (optional)
1 Tablespoon chopped fresh mint
⅓ cup red-wine vinegar; more as needed
1 cup extra-virgin olive oil; more as needed
   Kosher salt and freshly ground black pepper

For the brochettes:

4 pounds lamb shoulder or stew meat, cut into pieces of uniform size, about 2-inch cubes
   Olive oil for brushing
   Kosher salt and freshly ground black pepper

Make the vinaigrette—On a cutting board, mince together the garlic, capers, and olives. Transfer to a mixing bowl. Stir in the shallots, mustard, marjoram, mint, and vinegar. Mix in the olive oil with a fork to make a loose vinaigrette—it does not need to be emulsified. Season with salt and pepper. Taste and add more oil or vinegar if necessary. Set aside.

Make the brochettes—Prepare the grill. In a mixing bowl, lightly coat the meat with the olive oil. Season with salt and pepper.

Skewer the lamb by folding or shaping each chunk of meat into a rounded cube. Thread three or four pieces on each skewer, leaving the meat near the pointed end rather than the middle of the skewer.

COOKING RIGHT

When threading the skewers, group similar-size pieces together for even cooking.

When the grill is hot (you should be able to hold your hand just above the grate for 1 second), use tongs to clean the grate with a lightly oiled paper towel.

Grill the brochettes, keeping the exposed ends of the skewers away from the hottest part of the fire if you're using bamboo. Turn the brochettes every 2 minutes; some will cook faster than others, so you may need to rotate the skewers to even out the grilling. The lamb is medium-rare when the cubes begin to resist pressure when touched, after about 8 minutes. Before serving, let the brochettes rest a moment to allow the juices to redistribute. Drizzle liberally with the vinaigrette.

—STEVE JOHNSON

COOKING RIGHT

Use your fingers or a chef's knife to pit olives. The pits of black, oil cured olives often slip right out with a pinch. If the olives are stubborn, press the side of a large chef's knife against the olive on a cutting board and give the knife a good whack. That should split the olive open.

FISH & SHELLFISH

Picture yourself at a fish counter looking through the glass at the gleaming specimens inside. What are you in the mood for? Will it be the bright, pink salmon with its strong flavor and silken texture? Or would you prefer the more delicate creamy white sea bass? Perhaps you want a more steak-like fish, something to take home and toss on the grill, say, tuna or swordfish. The point is that when you say you're having fish for dinner, it can mean just about anything—and you'll find ideas for it all here.

THE RECIPES

Sear-Roasted Salmon Fillets with Lemon-Ginger Butter

SERVES 4

COOKING RIGHT

Sear-roasting starts on the stove. Sear the salmon until it's nicely browned, give it a flip, and finish it in a hot oven.

Warming the lemon juice makes it easier to mix it into the softened butter.
Serve the fish on a bed of mashed potatoes with a side of sautéed spinach.

6 Tablespoons butter, well softened at room temperature
2 Tablespoons fresh lemon juice, warmed slightly
2 Tablespoons minced fresh ginger
2 Tablespoons snipped fresh chives
   Olive oil for the pan
4 salmon fillets (5 ounces each), skinned if you like, patted dry
   Salt and freshly ground black pepper

In a bowl, blend the butter, lemon juice, ginger, and chives well. Set aside at room temperature.

Heat the oven to 500°F. Set a large ovenproof skillet over medium-high heat and add just enough oil to make a light film. Sprinkle the salmon lightly with salt and pepper. When the oil is very hot, add the salmon, skin side up, and cook until nicely browned, about 1 minute. Flip the fish over and put the skillet in the oven. Roast for 2 minutes for medium rare; 4 minutes for medium well. Check for doneness with the tip of a knife. Remove the pan from the oven, transfer the fish to serving plates. Immediately top the salmon with a tablespoon or so of the lemon-ginger butter.

—ISABELLE ALEXANDRE

Baked Salmon
in Lemon-Tarragon Crème Fraîche

SERVES 4

The reduced pan juices from the salmon have a delicious tangy flavor similar to that of béarnaise sauce. Serve the salmon with spring peas or asparagus.

- 3 Tablespoons fresh lemon juice
- 2 teaspoons finely chopped fresh tarragon
- 8 ounces (1 scant cup) crème fraîche
- 4 Tablespoons unsalted butter; more for the parchment
- 2 Tablespoons minced shallot
- ½ cup dry vermouth
- 4 skinless salmon fillets (6 to 7 ounces each), preferably center-cut
  Kosher salt and freshly ground black pepper
  Minced fresh dill or chives for garnish

This creamy sauce tames and complements salmon's full flavor.

Heat the oven to 350°F. Cut a piece of parchment to fit inside a large ovenproof skillet or flameproof baking dish. Lightly butter one side of the parchment. Combine the lemon juice, tarragon, and crème fraîche and set aside. Melt 2 tablespoons of the butter in the pan or baking dish over medium-high heat. Add the shallot and vermouth and reduce to a glaze; remove from the heat. Season the fillets with salt and pepper and arrange in a single layer in the pan. Pour the crème fraîche mixture over the salmon, cover with the parchment, butter side down, and bake until the salmon is just opaque throughout, 18 to 20 minutes.

Transfer the salmon to a plate and keep warm. Put the pan over medium heat and reduce the sauce until it's thick enough to lightly coat a spoon. Remove from the heat, whisk in the remaining 2 tablespoons butter, and taste for salt and pepper. Put each salmon fillet on a warm dinner plate and spoon the sauce over each. Garnish with dill or chives.

—PERLA MEYERS

Salmon Brochettes with Sliced Fennel Vinaigrette

SERVES 8; YIELDS 1½ CUPS VINAIGRETTE

Serve these brochettes with a salad of arugula and red onion. The vinaigrette doubles as a salad dressing.

For the fennel vinaigrette:
- 1 clove garlic
- 2 anchovy fillets
- 1 Tablespoon capers, rinsed
- 1 teaspoon grainy mustard
- 2 shallots, thinly sliced
- ¼ medium bulb fennel, outer leaves removed, cored, and thinly sliced (crosswise)
- ½ teaspoon fresh thyme
- ½ teaspoon crushed fennel seeds
- ¼ teaspoon dried red chile flakes
- ⅓ cup fresh lemon juice; more as needed
- 1 cup extra-virgin olive oil
- Kosher salt and freshly ground black pepper

For the brochettes:
- 4 pounds fresh salmon fillet (skin on)
- Kosher salt
- Olive oil for brushing

Make the vinaigrette—On a cutting board, mince together the garlic, anchovies, and capers. Transfer to a bowl and add the mustard, shallots, fennel, thyme, fennel seeds, chile flakes, and lemon juice. Stir briefly. Mix in the olive oil with a fork. Season with salt and pepper. Taste the vinaigrette; it should be slightly acidic when used with grilled fish, so add more lemon juice if necessary. Let stand for at least 1 hour so the fennel softens and the flavors mingle.

COOKING AHEAD

You can make the vinaigrette and skewer the salmon hours ahead of cooking. Keep the fish covered and refrigerated.

Try to thread the skewer straight down the middle so it stays intact when it's time to turn during grilling.

COOKING RIGHT

Pull out the pin bones if need be. (The pin bones run down the center of the fillet and are easy to feel with your finger.) Use pliers or tweezers and pull them out at an angle to least disturb the flesh.

Make the brochettes—Prepare the grill. Cut the salmon crosswise into 1-inch-wide strips, 3 to 4 ounces each. Thread the skewers through the salmon strips: Starting at the tapered end, carefully pierce the flesh, pushing the skewer all the way through to the fat end until the point pokes through.

When the grill is just on the hot side of medium (you should be able to hold your hand just above the grate for 2 seconds), use tongs to clean the grate with a lightly oiled paper towel.

Season the salmon lightly with salt and brush lightly with olive oil. Put the brochettes on the grill, skin side down, keeping the exposed skewer ends away from the fire if you're using bamboo.

The salmon will cook quickly but not always at the same rate. Cook until the skin is crispy and it "releases" from the grill, 2 to 3 minutes. Turn the brochettes with tongs or a spatula and cook another minute. If necessary, turn again and cook another minute. The salmon is ready when the flesh feels firm and almost begins to flake apart. Put the brochettes on a platter and drizzle immediately with the vinaigrette.

—STEVE JOHNSON

COOKING RIGHT

To cut the ginger quickly into strips, stack the slices and use a very sharp knife.

COOK'S CHOICE

You can substitute cod or any other mild tasting, firm-fleshed fish. Just remember that the cooking time will vary slightly.

Poached Halibut in Hot & Sour Broth
SERVES 4

Serve this with a spoon for the broth.

2	Tablespoons soy sauce
4	halibut fillets, ½ pound each (about 1 inch thick)
1	quart homemade or low-salt canned chicken broth
¼	cup honey
3	Tablespoons tomato paste
2½	Tablespoons cider vinegar
12	quarter-size slices peeled fresh ginger, cut into thin strips
¼	teaspoon Tabasco
¼	cup sliced scallions (greens included)
¼	cup chopped fresh cilantro

Drizzle the soy sauce over both sides of the halibut fillets. Cover and refrigerate.

In a 12-inch sauté pan, combine the chicken broth, honey, tomato paste, vinegar, ginger, and Tabasco. Bring to a simmer over medium heat and cook gently for 12 minutes, stirring occasionally and skimming foam as necessary. Add the fillets, cover, and poach gently at a bare simmer over medium-low heat until the fillets are slightly firm to the touch and the centers are almost opaque (make a small slit with a knife to check), 6 to 8 minutes; the fish should be slightly undercooked at this point. Turn off the heat and let sit covered for another 2 minutes.

Divide the halibut and broth evenly among four shallow bowls. Sprinkle generously with the scallions and cilantro and serve.

—ARLENE JACOBS

Spice-Rubbed Fish Fillets
SERVES 3 TO 4

For a quick side dish, toss some couscous with tiny diced red pepper and scallion.

½ Tablespoon freshly ground black pepper
½ teaspoon paprika
½ teaspoon dried thyme
¼ teaspoon dry mustard
¼ teaspoon kosher salt
⅛ teaspoon ground cayenne
1 pound tilapia or sole fillets (about 4 fillets)
2 Tablespoons plus 2 teaspoons olive oil
2 Tablespoons unsalted butter
1 Tablespoon fresh lemon juice; more to taste

In a bowl, combine the pepper, paprika, thyme, mustard, salt, and cayenne. Brush both sides of the fish with 2 teaspoons of the oil and gently rub the spice mix all over the fish.

In a small skillet, heat the butter over medium heat until it's a deep brown, about 3 minutes; whisk in the lemon juice and keep warm.

Heat 1 tablespoon of the oil in a heavy nonstick skillet over medium-high heat. Add two of the fillets and cook about 2 minutes per side; transfer to a plate and tent with foil. Wipe the pan and repeat with the remaining oil and fish. Serve immediately, spooning the butter over the fish.

—JENNIFER BUSHMAN

HOW TO TELL WHEN FISH IS COOKED

"Ten minutes per inch," is the oft-quoted guideline for how long to cook fish, but in reality, it's more like 8 minutes per inch. (And for fish like tuna and salmon, which people have grown to enjoy medium rare or rare, it may be even less.) Since the worst offense is overcooking, begin checking for doneness sooner rather than later by using the tip of a small knife to peek at the fish's interior. The fish should not flake yet—keep in mind it will continue to cook off the heat—but it should show signs of firming. Most white fish, such as tilapia, sole, and cod, are considered done when they just turn opaque throughout. If your fillet is very thin, skip the knife test; it's done as soon as the outside turns opaque.

Cod Fillets with Mustard-Tarragon Crumb Crust

SERVES 2

Few dishes are as easy—or delicious—as fresh fish paired with a crispy coating. Use the same baking method described below for the recipes on the facing page.

- 4 Tablespoons coarse fresh breadcrumbs
- 1 Tablespoon chopped fresh tarragon
- ½ teaspoon grated lemon zest
- 2 teaspoons melted butter
  Salt and freshly ground black pepper
- 2 cod fillets, about 6 ounces each and 1 inch thick
- ½ teaspoon Dijon mustard

Heat the oven to 450°F. In a small bowl, gently mix the crumbs, tarragon, lemon zest, melted butter, and a little salt and pepper.

Spread each fillet with ¼ teaspoon mustard and season with more salt and pepper. Carefully pat the crumb topping over the surface of each fillet, pressing lightly so it sticks.

Brush a little oil onto a small baking sheet or shallow baking pan and set the fillets on the oiled spot (or use a nonstick pan). Bake the fish in the hot oven until the topping is golden brown and crisp and the fish is tender all the way through when you poke it with a thin knife or a skewer, 10 to 15 minutes. If the topping seems like it's going to burn before the fish is done, turn the heat down to 375°F. Serve immediately.

—MARTHA HOLMBERG

COOKING RIGHT

To make coarse fresh bread-crumbs, pulse pieces of day-old bread (whatever you have on hand, even pitas and English muffins make great breadcrumbs) in a food processor until just crumbly.

MORE FISH TOPPINGS

Bake the fish under these tasty toppings in the manner described in the recipe on the facing page.

Salmon Fillets with Horseradish-Potato Crust

SERVES 2

1 small boiling potato, boiled until just tender, chilled, and peeled
  Salt and freshly ground black pepper
2 teaspoons oil or melted butter
1½ teaspoons prepared horseradish
2 salmon fillets, about 6 ounces each and 1 inch thick

Heat the oven to 400°F. Grate the potato thinly using the large holes of a box grater. Season with salt and pepper and toss with the oil or melted butter.

Spread half the horseradish on each fillet and season with a little more salt and pepper. Gently pat the potato topping on the surface of each fillet, pressing lightly so it sticks.

Bake according to the instructions in the recipe on the facing page, but note the lower temperature in this recipe. Cook the fish for 15 to 18 minutes. If the fish is almost cooked but the potato topping isn't crisp, switch the oven to broil for the last few minutes. Serve immediately.

Halibut Fillets with Pine Nut & Parmesan Crust

SERVES 2

4 Tablespoons pine nuts, chopped
2 Tablespoons grated fresh Parmesan or Asiago
¼ teaspoon minced garlic
2 teaspoons chopped fresh herbs (such as a mix of basil, mint, and sage)
  Tiny pinch cayenne
2 teaspoons olive oil
2 halibut fillets, about 6 ounces each and 1 inch thick
  Salt

Heat the oven to 450°F. In a small bowl, gently mix the chopped pine nuts, Parmesan, garlic, herbs, cayenne, and olive oil.

Season the fish with a little salt. Carefully pat the nut topping over the surface of each fillet, pressing lightly so it sticks. Bake according to the instructions in the recipe on the facing page. ◆

Caramel-Braised Cod

SERVES 4

A quick caramel sauce adds a deep, toasty flavor to the fish while scallions add a bright burst of flavor and color; it's a winning combination. Serve the cod with fragrant jasmine rice to further enjoy the flavor of the sauce.

1 teaspoon crushed red pepper flakes
¼ teaspoon salt
¼ cup plus 1 teaspoon sugar
1½ pounds cod fillets, 1 inch thick
2 Tablespoons olive oil
3 Tablespoons fish sauce
1 scallion (white and light green parts), thinly sliced

Combine the red pepper flakes, salt, and 1 teaspoon sugar in a small bowl. Rub the fish with half of the mixture and set aside. Combine the other half of the mixture with ¼ cup water, the oil, and the fish sauce; set aside.

Put the remaining ¼ cup sugar in a large, heavy-based sauté pan with straight sides and cook over high heat until the sugar starts to melt at the edges and turns golden brown, about 2 minutes. Reduce the heat to medium when the sugar starts browning and stir energetically with a wooden spoon. When the caramel is a reddish mahogany brown (another 1 to 2 minutes), take the pan off the heat. Stirring gently, slowly add ½ cup water to the pan; be careful, as the caramel may steam or spatter. If the caramel doesn't dissolve completely, return the pan to medium heat and stir until dissolved. Stir in the fish sauce mixture.

Put the fish in a single layer in the sauté pan. Bring to a gentle simmer over medium-low heat and braise the fish, uncovered; use a soupspoon to baste the fish with the sauce occasionally. After about 7 minutes, gently flip the fish and continue to braise and baste until the fish is opaque throughout, another 5 to 7 minutes. Serve with the sauce and sprinkled with the scallions.

—KIM LANDI

Cod Stew with Chorizo, Leeks & Potatoes

SERVES 4

Here is a hearty fish stew with enough spice to warm up a winter evening. Chorizo, a Spanish smoked pork, is sold in many supermarkets.

2 small leeks (or 1 large leek), white and light green
   parts only

6 ounces chorizo

1 pound red potatoes (4 to 5 medium),
   scrubbed and cut into ¾-inch cubes
   Kosher salt and freshly ground black pepper

1 Tablespoon olive oil

3 cloves garlic, minced

1 can (28 ounces) diced tomatoes, with their juices

½ cup dry white wine

¼ cup chopped fresh flat-leaf parsley

1 pound cod fillet, cut into 4 even portions

Chop the leeks into ½-inch pieces and rinse thoroughly to remove all the grit. Cut the chorizo in half lengthwise and slice into half moons about ⅛ inch thick.

Boil the potatoes in ample, well-salted water until tender, 10 to 15 minutes; drain.

While the potatoes cook, heat the oil in a large pot over medium heat for 1 minute. Add the chorizo and leeks and cook, stirring occasionally, until the chorizo has browned slightly and the leeks are soft, about 6 minutes. Add the garlic and cook for 1 minute. Stir in the tomatoes and their juices, the wine, 1½ cups water, and ½ teaspoon salt. Bring to a boil over high heat. Partially cover the pot, reduce the heat to medium, and simmer for 15 minutes. Add the potatoes, season with salt and pepper, and stir in half of the parsley. Season the cod with salt and pepper, set the fillets on top of the stew, cover, and simmer until just cooked through, 6 to 8 minutes. Carefully transfer the cod to shallow soup bowls (the fillets may break apart). Spoon the stew over the cod, garnish with the remaining parsley, and serve.

—EVA KATZ

COOKING RIGHT

For a good-looking presentation, cut the sausage lengthwise in half and then slice it into half moons about ⅛ inch thick.

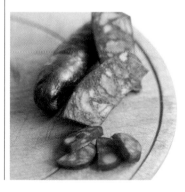

COOK'S CHOICE

You can substitute chicken breast or pork tenderloin in place of the fish.

COOKING RIGHT

Use the bulb end of lemongrass. Peel away the fibrous outer layer and trim the root end. Slice the bulb into very thin rounds first to make chopping easier.

Seared Sea Bass with Spicy Lemongrass Crust
SERVES 4

Because of the demand by cooks smitten with the exciting flavors of Thai cooking, you can now find items like curry paste and lemongrass in the supermarket.

For the marinade:

¼ cup finely chopped lemongrass (1 to 2 stalks)
2 teaspoons dried chile flakes; more to taste
1 Tablespoon finely chopped garlic
½ teaspoon turmeric
1½ teaspoons kosher salt
2 teaspoons sugar
4 sea bass fillets, 6 ounces each
2 to 3 Tablespoons vegetable oil

For the sauce:

¾ cup unsweetened coconut milk
1½ teaspoons green curry paste
⅔ cup homemade or low-salt canned chicken stock
1 Tablespoon fish sauce
1 Tablespoon sugar
¼ teaspoon turmeric

In a bowl, combine the lemongrass, chile flakes, garlic, turmeric, salt, sugar, and 2 tablespoons water. Add the sea bass, turning to cover it, and marinate for about 20 minutes.

In a small saucepan, heat 3 tablespoons of the coconut milk over low heat. Add the curry paste and cook, stirring to dissolve, for a minute. Add the chicken stock, remaining coconut milk, fish sauce, sugar, and turmeric. Simmer until slightly reduced, about 10 minutes, and keep warm. In a large nonstick frying pan, heat the oil over medium-high heat. Add the fillets and cook until just done, 5 to 6 minutes on each side. Drain on paper towels and serve in a pool of the curry sauce.

—MAI PHAM

Grilled Tuna with Mango & Habanero Sauce

SERVES 4

The sweet and spicy flavors in the sauce are a perfect foil for the grilled tuna. Snap or snow peas would add even more color as a side dish.

For the tuna and marinade:

- ¼ cup finely chopped fresh flat-leaf parsley
- ½ cup finely chopped fresh cilantro, plus whole leaves for garnish
- 2 cloves garlic, minced
- ¼ cup dry sherry
- ¼ cup olive oil
  Kosher salt and freshly ground black pepper
- 4 tuna steaks, 6 ounces each

For *the sauce*:

- 1 ripe, juicy mango, peeled and pitted
- ¼ cup Chardonnay or other dry white wine
  Juice of ½ orange (about ¼ cup)
- ½ to ¾ teaspoon minced habanero, Scotch bonnet, or other hot chile (seeds removed)

Make the marinade—In a large shallow dish, mix the parsley, cilantro, garlic, sherry, olive oil, 1 teaspoon salt, and pepper. Add the tuna and toss to thoroughly coat, pressing the herbs all over the steaks. Let sit for 30 minutes.

Make the sauce—In a blender, combine the mango, Chardonnay, and orange juice. Stir in the habanero and set aside.

Cook the tuna—Prepare the grill. When hot, remove the tuna from the marinade and season it with salt and pepper. Sear the tuna for 3 to 5 minutes on each side for medium rare (or more, depending on the thickness of the tuna). Drizzle some sauce on each plate, set the tuna on the sauce, drizzle on a little more sauce, and garnish with cilantro.

—NORMAN VAN AKEN

COOK'S CHOICE

The floral note of the hot habanero partners well with the mango, but if you can't find habanero, substitute another spicy chile. The flavors in this dish are also delicious with grilled pork or shrimp.

Broiled Swordfish with Browned Butter-Red Pepper Sauce

SERVES 4

You could just as easily grill the swordfish in about the same time as it takes to broil.

4 swordfish steaks (2 pounds total), each about 1 inch thick
⅓ cup extra-virgin olive oil
4 cloves garlic, minced, plus 6 large cloves, thickly sliced
  Large pinch crushed red chile flakes
⅓ cup minced fresh flat-leaf parsley
2 Tablespoons fresh lemon juice
  Freshly ground black pepper
6 Tablespoons unsalted butter
1 jar (12 ounces) roasted red peppers, drained and sliced into thin strips
¼ cup drained tiny capers, rinsed
  Kosher salt
1 Tablespoon balsamic vinegar

Heat the broiler with the rack as close to the heat source as possible.

Arrange the fish steaks in a 9x13-inch baking dish. Combine the oil, garlic, chile flakes, half of the parsley, the lemon juice, and a generous amount of pepper. Coat the steaks with this mixture.

Melt the butter in a large skillet over medium heat until bubbling; reduce the heat to medium low and cook the butter until it begins to turn light brown, about 2 minutes. Add the sliced garlic and cook, stirring occasionally, until it turns golden, another 2 to 3 minutes. Stir in the peppers and capers and take the pan off the heat.

Season the fish with salt and put it on a cold broiler pan. Broil, turning once, until cooked through, about 10 minutes. Meanwhile, reheat the sauce over medium heat until it's sizzling. Stir in the balsamic vinegar, the remaining parsley, and black pepper. When hot, spoon this mixture on top of the fish and serve immediately.

—LAUREN GROVEMAN

Seared Scallops with Pineapple-Ginger Sauce

SERVES 4

Choose "dry scallops," which have not been treated with STP, a preservative that gives scallops a longer shelf-life but also gives them a rubbery texture and makes them nearly impossible to brown.

- 6 Tablespoons homemade or low-salt canned chicken broth
- ¼ cup thawed pineapple juice concentrate
- ½ teaspoon grated fresh ginger
- 1½ pounds sea scallops, patted dry
- 2 Tablespoons olive oil
  Coarse salt and freshly ground black pepper
- 1 Tablespoon unsalted butter

Combine the chicken broth, pineapple juice concentrate, and ginger in a small bowl. Set the scallops on a plate and drizzle with the oil; turn to coat. Sprinkle both sides with salt and pepper. About 2 minutes before searing the scallops, set a heavy-based 12-inch nonstick skillet over high heat and turn on the exhaust fan.

When the pan is very hot, add the scallops. Cook over high heat until they develop an even, rich brown crust, 2 to 3 minutes per side. Remove from the heat and transfer the scallops to a plate.

Return the empty skillet to the heat and add the pineapple juice mixture; boil until the liquid reduces by about half. Tilting the skillet so that the reduced liquid is at one side of the pan, whisk in the butter. Spoon a portion of the sauce over the scallops and serve immediately.

—PAM ANDERSON

COOKING RIGHT

To get rid of the tough abductor muscle on a scallop, just peel if off.

COOKING RIGHT

For this recipe, don't use "easy-peel" shrimp as too much salt would get into the shrimp meat. If you must use "easy-peel" shrimp, cut the salt in half. Also, big shrimp do best on the grill as they are less apt to overcook.

Salt & Pepper Crusted Shrimp with Two Dipping Sauces

SERVES 4

Serve the shrimp in the shells to peel with your fingers and dip into the sauces.

For the lemon-basil dipping sauce:

    Finely grated zest and juice of 1 large lemon
1 large clove garlic, smashed and peeled
½ cup best-quality extra-virgin olive oil
8 large fresh basil leaves, chopped

For the butter sauce:

4 Tablespoons unsalted butter, melted
2 teaspoons Worcestershire sauce
    Garlic powder

For the shrimp:

2 pounds jumbo shrimp in the shell (24 to 30, not "easy-peel"), thawed completely if frozen and blotted dry
2 Tablespoons olive oil
2 Tablespoons kosher salt
1½ teaspoons coarsely ground black pepper

Heat a gas grill to medium high or prepare a medium-hot charcoal fire. While the grill is heating, make the sauces. For the lemon-basil sauce, combine all the ingredients in a small bowl and mix well. For the butter sauce, put the melted butter in a small heatproof bowl. Stir in the Worcestershire sauce and several shakes of garlic powder.

When the grill is hot, blot the shrimp dry and put them in a large bowl. Toss with the oil to coat lightly. Immediately before grilling, mix the salt and pepper and sprinkle evenly over the shrimp; toss to coat thoroughly. Put the shrimp directly on the grate and grill, turning once, until the shells are pink and the flesh is opaque. Serve with the sauces.

—ELIZABETH KARMEL

Stir-Fried Shrimp, Sugar Snaps & Fennel

SERVES 6

Because the garlic and ginger are grated so fine, they are added later than usual for a stir-fry and cooked just long enough to get rid of the raw flavor.

For the fennel oil:

2½ tablespoons fennel seeds, finely ground

¼ cup extra-virgin olive oil

For the stir-fry:

½ pound sugar snap peas, trimmed

1 teaspoon kosher salt

1 cup thinly sliced (about ⅛ inch) fennel

2 pounds jumbo shrimp (16 to 20 per pound), shelled and deveined

1 teaspoon finely grated garlic

1 teaspoon finely grated fresh ginger

2 Tablespoons very thinly sliced fresh mint

1 lime, sliced into wedges

At least a day ahead, make the oil—Moisten the ground fennel seed with a few drops of water so that it adheres to itself slightly when squeezed. Stir together the moistened ground fennel and olive oil. Seal and refrigerate overnight or up to a week. Before using, warm the oil to room temperature and strain through cheesecloth.

In a large sauté pan or stir-fry pan, heat 3 tablespoons of the fennel oil over medium-high heat (the oil is hot enough when you put a sugar snap in the pan and it starts to sizzle). Add the sugar snaps, season with some of the salt, and stir-fry until the peas have a bit of a golden color and are crunchy and blistery, about 2 minutes. Add the fennel, season with a bit more salt, and stir-fry until the fennel is al dente, about 60 seconds.

Increase the heat to high, add the shrimp, toss well, and make a space in the center of the pan. Into this space, pour the remaining fennel oil and then add the garlic and ginger, stirring for about 15 seconds. Season with a bit more salt and continue to stir-fry until the shrimp are no longer glossy and start to look pink. Taste and add more salt if you like, scatter the mint on top, and serve with the lime wedges on the side.

—GARY DANKO

COOKING AHEAD

The fennel oil will gain in flavor the longer it sits. A day ahead is fine, but a few days would be even better.

COOKING RIGHT

To remove the tough fiber on a snap pea, use your fingernail to snap off the stem end toward the top seam, leaving the stringy part attached. Pull on the disconnected stem end like a zipper pull and pull off the string as you would unzip a zipper.

BEANS & GRAINS

When your main course is simply prepared—a grilled steak, roast chicken, seared tuna—you want a side dish that adds tons of flavor and wonderful texture. All of the recipes here do that. (Many add color, too.) In this chapter, you'll learn how to tailor rice pilaf to suit the meal (and your mood) and how to cook beans to their tender best. Couscous, though technically not a grain (it's more like a tiny pasta), is included here because it gets treated like a grain in these fragrant and pretty side dishes.

THE RECIPES

White Beans with Rosemary & Olive Oil

Roasted Garlic & White Bean Purée

Black Beans with Mango, Citrus & Crunchy Jícama

Chickpea, Carrot & Parsley Salad

Lemon Rice Salad

Green Rice

Wild Rice with Dried Apricots & Pine Nuts

Basic Rice Pilaf

Tabbouleh Salad with Slow-Roasted Tomatoes

Wheatberries with Fragrant Spices, Currants & Almonds

Couscous with Ginger, Orange, Almond & Herbs

Couscous with Cilantro & Melted Scallions

White Beans with Rosemary & Olive Oil

YIELDS ABOUT 8 CUPS

This recipe works well with any large, meaty bean. Serve the dish warm or at room temperature. It could accompany grilled tuna and tomatoes in summer or lamb chops with radicchio in the winter.

1 pound large dried white beans, such as cannellini or Giant Aztec
1 large onion, peeled and quartered
1 head garlic, cloves separated but not peeled
   Sprigs of fresh rosemary, thyme, and sage
2 Tablespoons extra-virgin olive oil; more for garnish
2 teaspoons salt
1 teaspoon ground fennel seeds
1 teaspoon dried red pepper flakes
   Freshly ground black pepper
   Chopped fresh rosemary for garnish

Pick over the beans. Soak if desired and drain. In a large, heavy-based pot, cover the beans with 8 cups cold water. Add the onion, garlic, and herb sprigs and bring to a boil over high heat. Reduce the heat to a bare simmer, skimming any foam that rises to the surface. When the beans are almost tender, after about 1 hour, add the olive oil, salt, ground fennel, and pepper flakes. Continue cooking until the beans are very tender but still whole, about 30 minutes longer. Taste the beans and broth; add more salt if necessary. Allow the beans to cool in the broth for at least 1 hour before serving.

To serve, warm the beans in the broth, and then transfer the beans to a platter with a slotted spoon, discarding the onion, garlic, and herb sprigs. Garnish with a drizzle of olive oil, a few grindings of black pepper, and the chopped rosemary.

—DAVID TANIS

COOKING RIGHT

Give beans a long soak for the best results. Beans soaked at least 8 hours will cook up more plump and tender and in a shorter time. Drain the soaking water and begin the cooking with fresh water.

Roasted Garlic & White Bean Purée

YIELDS 4½ CUPS; SERVES 6

This flavorful purée makes a great bed on which to rest some braised lamb shanks or other meaty, saucy dish.

2 cups dried white beans, such as Great Northern, soaked overnight in cold water and drained

1 whole head garlic

1 Tablespoon olive oil

½ teaspoon chopped fresh thyme

½ cup heavy cream, warmed

1¾ teaspoons salt

   Freshly ground black pepper

Put the drained beans in a large saucepan and add water to cover the beans by 3 inches. Bring to a boil, cover, and simmer until very tender, 1 to 1½ hours. Meanwhile, heat the oven to 400°F. Cut off the top third of the garlic head to expose the cloves. Coat the cut side with the olive oil, wrap the garlic loosely in foil, set on a baking sheet, and roast until soft, about 1 hour.

Drain the cooked beans; put them in a food processor. Squeeze about 8 of the roasted cloves of garlic into the bowl. (The rest of the garlic will keep, wrapped, for about a week in the refrigerator.) Add the thyme and half of the warmed cream and purée. Add just enough of the remaining cream while pulsing until the purée is the consistency of mashed potatoes. Season with salt and pepper.

—DEBRA PONZEK

COOK'S CHOICE

For an even richer purée, warm ¼ cup mascarpone cheese with ¼ cup milk and add that to the beans in place of the cream and pulse.

COOKING AHEAD

The garlic can be roasted ahead of time; it will keep for about a week in the refrigerator. In fact, since roasted garlic is so delicious, you may as well roast a couple of heads to have extra on hand for pasta sauces, vinaigrettes, or to smear on toasted bread.

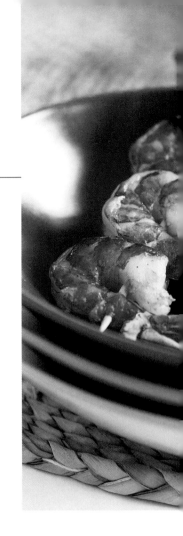

Black Beans with Mango, Citrus & Crunchy Jícama

SERVES 4 TO 6

The canned chipotle chile is a smoked, dried jalapeño that's canned in a spicy sauce called adobo. Look for it in the Mexican foods section of your grocery store. To tell if a mango is ripe, press on it to be sure it gives a little. To make this salad using dried beans requires a little more time, but you will be rewarded with a more flavorful result. Good quality canned beans, however, will also work well.

For the beans:

1   cup dried black beans, cooked (see recipe at left), or 1 can (29 ounces) black beans

For the dressing:

1   teaspoon finely grated orange zest
¼   cup fresh orange juice
1   teaspoon finely grated lime zest
¼   cup fresh lime juice
2   teaspoons sugar
1   teaspoon finely minced canned chipotle in adobo sauce, seeded
1   teaspoon minced garlic
½   teaspoon kosher salt
¼   teaspoon freshly ground black pepper

To assemble:

1   ripe mango, cut into ¼-inch dice (about 1⅓ cups)
1   cup ¼-inch diced jícama (about half of a 2-pound jícama)
2   tablespoons minced red onion
¼   cup finely sliced fresh basil
3   Tablespoons extra-virgin olive oil

COOKING RIGHT

The beans will absorb the most flavor if you toss them with the other ingredients while they are still warm.

Cooked Black Beans

1   cup dried black beans, rinsed and picked over and soaked overnight if desired
1½ teaspoons kosher salt
¼   small onion
4   4-inch basil stems

Put the beans in a large pot, cover with 3 to 4 inches of water, add the salt, onion, and basil stems, and bring to a boil. Reduce to a simmer and cook until the beans are very tender but not falling apart. The time will vary from 45 minutes to 1½ hours or longer. Cool the cooked beans in their liquid for 15 minutes and then drain.

Cook the dried beans following the method described on the facing page. Transfer them to a large bowl and keep them warm. (If using canned beans, rinse and drain well.)

Whisk together the orange zest and juice, the lime zest and juice, the sugar, chipotle, garlic, salt, and pepper until the sugar has dissolved. Toss the dressing with the warm cooked or canned beans, using a rubber spatula to gently fold so the beans get well coated but not smashed. Let the beans sit for a few minutes and then toss a few more times. It may seem like too much liquid at first, but the beans will gradually absorb it all. Fold in the mango, jícama, onion, basil, and olive oil and serve.

—MARTHA HOLMBERG

COOKING AHEAD

You can make this bean salad ahead of time and keep it refrigerated, but be sure to let the salad come to room temperature before serving it to let the flavors blossom and the beans become nice and tender again. Taste and season if necessary.

TRY JÍCAMA FOR SALAD OR SNACKS

Jícama (pronounced HEE-kah-mah) is a softball-sized tuber with a rough, papery brown skin. Although you may have walked right by it, many supermarkets now carry it in the produce section. (It only needs to be refrigerated after it's been cut.) Jícama, which is often used in Mexican cooking, has a crisp, juicy flesh, sort of like an apple—but it's not sweet. Peel off not only its skin, but also a thin (⅛-inch) layer of the flesh, which can be a bit fibrous. Once peeled, it's easy to slice and dice. For a refreshing snack, try slicing jícama into sticks and sprinkling the sticks with lime juice, chile powder, and salt. Jícama also adds a welcome crunch to salsa, green salads, and sandwiches.

Chickpea, Carrot & Parsley Salad

SERVES 4 TO 6 AS A VEGETARIAN MAIN DISH;
8 AS A SIDE DISH

COOKING AHEAD

If you want to make this in advance, combine the salad ingredients and make the dressing, but don't mix them together until ready to serve.

Canned chickpeas are a great convenience food, and they make a substantial vegetarian meal. Serve the salad with toasted pita wedges.

1 can (19 ounces) chickpeas, drained and rinsed
1 cup loosely packed fresh flat-leaf parsley leaves, very coarsely chopped
1 cup loosely packed shredded carrot (from about 1 large carrot)
½ cup sliced radishes (about 6 medium)
½ cup chopped scallions, white and green parts (about 4)
3 Tablespoons fresh lemon juice
1 teaspoon ground coriander
   Kosher salt and freshly ground black pepper
6 Tablespoons extra-virgin olive oil
⅓ cup crumbled feta or toasted pine nuts (optional)

Put ½ cup of the chickpeas in a mixing bowl and mash them into a coarse paste with a potato masher or large wooden spoon. Toss in the remaining chickpeas along with the parsley, carrot, radishes, and scallions. Stir to combine.

COOKING RIGHT

Use a box grater or a mini food processor to shred the carrot.

In a liquid measuring cup, whisk together the lemon juice, coriander, ½ teaspoon salt, and a few generous grinds of black pepper. Continue whisking while adding the olive oil in a slow stream. Pour over the salad and toss gently. Season the salad with salt and pepper. Top with the feta or pine nuts, if using, and serve immediately.

—MOLLY STEVENS

Lemon Rice Salad

YIELDS ABOUT 5 CUPS

A fresh lemon-herb dressing pairs well with the nutty flavor of basmati rice. Cool and gently fluff the basmati before dressing to ensure a light salad.

¼ cup minced shallots or scallions (white and green parts)

2 Tablespoons olive oil

1 cup basmati or jasmine rice, well rinsed

2 cups vegetable or chicken stock

1 teaspoon grated lemon zest

2½ Tablespoons fresh lemon juice

⅓ cup roughly chopped cilantro, basil, mint, or a mix

1 teaspoon finely minced garlic

½ cup finely diced red onion, rinsed in cold water

½ cup diced red bell pepper

⅓ cup lightly toasted pine nuts, pepitas, or chopped cashews

In a deep saucepan over moderate heat, sauté the shallots in 1 tablespoon of the olive oil until soft but not brown. Add the rice and continue to sauté for 2 to 3 minutes longer, stirring regularly. Add the stock and bring to a boil. Reduce the heat to a simmer, cover, and continue to cook until all the liquid is absorbed, 14 to 16 minutes. Remove from the heat and let stand, partially covered, for 5 minutes. Gently fluff the rice with a fork and pour into a large bowl to cool completely.

Add the lemon zest, juice, herbs, garlic, onion, bell pepper, nuts, and remaining 1 tablespoon of olive oil to the rice and gently stir to combine. If not using immediately, cover and refrigerate for up to 3 days.

—JOHN ASH

COOK'S CHOICE

Pine nuts and cashews work great in the salad, but for a delicious twist, seek out pepitas, which are dark-green hulled pumpkin seeds. (If they're not at the grocery store, try a natural-foods store.)

Green Rice

SERVES 6 TO 8

Rich and refined, "arroz verde" has a deep gorgeous color and a buttery, herbal flavor that's just as delicious alongside a grilled steak as it is when paired more traditionally with Mexican food.

½ cup tightly packed fresh cilantro sprigs (about ½ ounce)
1 cup tightly packed fresh stemmed spinach leaves (about 1½ ounces)
1¼ cups homemade or low-salt canned chicken stock
1¼ cups milk
1 teaspoon salt
1 Tablespoon olive oil
3 Tablespoons unsalted butter
1½ cups long-grain rice
¼ cup finely minced onion
1 clove garlic, minced

Put the cilantro, spinach, and stock in a blender and blend until the greens are puréed. Add the milk and salt and blend a bit more until well combined.

Heat the olive oil and butter in a medium-sized (3-quart) heavy-based saucepan with a good lid over medium heat. When the butter is melted, add the rice and sauté, stirring about every 30 seconds, until it just begins to brown, 3 to 4 minutes. Add the onion and garlic and cook 1 minute, stirring constantly. Add the contents of the blender, stir well, turn the heat to high, and bring to a boil. Cover the pan, turn the heat to very low, and cook for 20 minutes. Stir the rice carefully to avoid crushing it, cover, and cook another 5 minutes. Take the pan off the heat and let the rice steam in the covered pot for 10 minutes. Serve hot.

—JIM PEYTON

COOKING AHEAD

You can prepare the cooking liquid mixture earlier in the day and keep it refrigerated. When it comes time to make the rice, the dish comes together in a snap.

Wild Rice with Dried Apricots & Pine Nuts

SERVES 4

Wild rice varies, so check for doneness after 45 minutes, but it may need more than an hour. Try this rice with one of the glazed pork tenderloin recipes on p. 121 or with the turkey cutlets on p. 101.

3 Tablespoons butter
1 medium onion, diced
1 teaspoon finely chopped fresh rosemary
1 cup wild rice
2 cups homemade or low-salt canned chicken stock
¾ teaspoon salt
⅓ cup diced dried apricots
½ cup toasted pine nuts
  Freshly ground black pepper

In a medium-sized frying pan, heat the butter over medium heat and sauté the onion and rosemary until the onion is deep golden, about 10 minutes. Add the wild rice and stir to coat. Add the stock and salt. Cover, bring to a boil, and reduce the heat. Simmer over medium-low heat until the grains are slightly open and tender but not mushy, about 50 minutes. Let rest, covered, for 5 minutes. Stir in the apricots, pine nuts, and pepper; taste and adjust seasonings.

—AMANDA CUSHMAN

COOK'S CHOICE

Try dried cherries or cranberries instead of apricots and brown rice instead of wild.

COOKING RIGHT

Lighter stocks like chicken or veal are best for cooking pilafs.

Basic Rice Pilaf

SERVES 4

Use this method to make plain rice pilaf, to make one of the variations listed on the facing page, or to create your own inspired dish.

2 Tablespoons oil
  or butter
⅓ cup finely chopped onion or shallots
1 cup long-grain white rice
2 cups broth or other liquid
½ teaspoon kosher salt

Heat the butter or oil in a heavy-based 2- or 3-quart saucepan over medium-low heat. Add the onion or shallots as desired or as recipe directs plus any other "start" ingredients listed in the variation recipes at right and cook, stirring, until softened but not browned. Stir in the rice and any seasonings and cook for about 1 minute. Pour in the 2 cups chicken broth or the combination of broth and other liquids. Add the salt and any fruits or hardy herbs. Increase the heat to high and boil, uncovered, until the level of the liquid is just above the level of the rice and you can see air holes forming in the rice, about 5 minutes. Cover immediately, reduce the heat to low, and simmer (or bake in a 350°F oven) for exactly 15 minutes, without lifting the lid. Let the rice rest for at least 5 minutes (and up to 20 minutes) off the heat. Don't uncover until after the first 5 minutes of resting. Fluff and separate the rice grains with a fork. (Don't stir vigorously or the rice may get gummy.) Fold in any final flavorings and then taste and add salt and pepper as needed.

—JENNIFER ARMENTROUT

COOKING RIGHT

Boil the rice for longer than you think you should. Don't turn down the heat until you see these signs: The level of the liquid is just above the rice and air holes in the rice are forming.

CONTEMPORARY PILAFS

To make these variations add or substitute the ingredients listed below when they are called for in the basic recipe on the facing page.

Curried Coconut Pilaf

To start: Butter, onion. Seasoning: 1½ teaspoon curry powder. **Liquid:** 1¼ cups "lite" coconut milk mixed with ¾ cup chicken broth. **Fruit:** 2 tablespoon currants. **Final flavorings:** ¼ cup toasted sliced almonds, 2 tablespoons chopped fresh cilantro.

Lemon-Dill Pilaf

To start: butter, onion. **Seasoning:** ½ teaspoon ground coriander. **Liquid:** 1¾ cups chicken broth combined with 2 tablespoons each fresh lemon juice and dry white wine. **Hardy herb:** one bay leaf.

Final flavorings: 1½ tablespoons chopped fresh dill and 1 teaspoon grated lemon zest.

Creole Pilaf

To start: olive oil, onion, ⅓ cup finely chopped green pepper, 1 chopped garlic clove. **Seasoning:** 1 teaspoon ground cumin, 1 table-spoon paprika. **Liquid:** juice drained from a 14-ounce can diced tomatoes (reserve the tomatoes) mixed with broth to make 2 cups). **Fruit:** Reserved canned tomatoes. **Final flavoring:** 2 tablespoons chopped fresh parsley or sliced scallions.

Mushroom Pilaf

To start: butter, shallots, 4 dried shiitake mushrooms reconstituted in chicken broth, drained (liquid reserved), and finely chopped. **Liquid:** reserved mushroom soaking liquid plus more broth to equal 2 cups. **Hardy herb:** a sprig of fresh thyme. **Final flavoring:** 1 Tablespoon chopped fresh tarragon. ◆

Tabbouleh Salad with Slow-Roasted Tomatoes
SERVES 4 TO 6

COOKING AHEAD

The tomatoes can be cooked a day or two ahead and refrigerated. Before serving, bring them to room temperature.

COOKING RIGHT

Cook bulgur until it feels al dente or it will end up mushy in the salad. Taste it as it nears the end of its cooking time and take it off the heat while it still has a little bite.

The California hook in this traditional Middle Eastern salad is the sweet and caramelized roasted tomatoes. They're a perfect foil for the lemony-herby tabbouleh.

For the tomatoes:
3 pounds ripe medium tomatoes, halved and gently seeded
3 Tablespoons olive oil
Salt and freshly ground black pepper

For the salad:
⅓ cup fine bulgur wheat
⅓ cup vegetable stock, chicken stock, or water, heated to boiling
¼ cup olive oil
1½ cups finely chopped fresh flat-leaf parsley
¼ cup finely chopped fresh mint
2 Tablespoons minced scallion (white and green parts)
1 Tablespoon finely minced garlic
3 Tablespoons fresh lemon juice
2 teaspoons finely grated lemon zest
¼ cup toasted pine nuts
Fresh mint sprigs

Roast the tomatoes—Heat the oven to 350°F. Coat the tomatoes with the olive oil, season with salt and pepper, and arrange them, cut side down, on a rimmed baking sheet. Roast the tomatoes until very concentrated and browned, with most of their juices cooked off, about 2½ hours.

Make the salad—In a bowl, combine the bulgur, stock, and half the olive oil; cover and let stand for at least 30 minutes. Uncover, fluff with a fork, and stir in the remaining olive oil, parsley, mint, scallion, garlic, lemon juice, and zest. Taste and add salt and pepper as needed. Mound the tabbouleh in the middle of each plate and arrange the roasted tomatoes around the tabbouleh. Garnish with the pine nuts and sprigs of mint.

—JOHN ASH

Wheatberries with Fragrant Spices, Currants & Almonds

SERVES 4 TO 6 AS A SIDE DISH

You can serve the wheatberries like a pilaf as a side dish or you can use them to stuff poultry or vegetables such as baked red peppers and tomatoes.

½ cup wheatberries, soaked for 4 hours
    or overnight
    Salt
2 Tablespoons olive oil or unsalted butter
½ medium onion, chopped into medium dice
4 scallions (white and light green parts only), chopped
¼ teaspoon ground allspice
¼ teaspoon ground cinnamon
½ cup basmati or other long-grain white rice
⅓ cup dried currants or coarsely chopped raisins
¾ cup homemade or low-salt canned chicken or vegetable broth
1½ ounces (⅓ cup) slivered almonds, toasted
2 Tablespoons chopped fresh flat-leaf parsley
1 Tablespoon grated lemon zest
    Freshly ground black pepper

Drain the wheatberries. In a small saucepan, bring the wheatberries and 3 cups salted water to a boil. Reduce the heat to low, cover, and simmer until tender but pleasantly chewy, 25 to 50 minutes. Drain well.

Meanwhile, heat the oil or butter in a small saucepan over medium low. Add the onion and scallions; cook until tender and translucent, about 7 minutes. Stir in the allspice, cinnamon, and rice, cook until the spices are fragrant, 1 to 2 minutes, then add the currants or raisins, the broth, and salt. Bring to a boil, turn the heat to low, cover, and simmer until the liquid is just absorbed and the rice is tender, 12 to 15 minutes.

In a bowl, combine the wheatberries, rice mixture, and almonds. Stir in the parsley and lemon zest and adjust the salt, pepper, and cinnamon.

—JOYCE GOLDSTEIN

COOKING RIGHT

Wheatberries are either hard or soft, but they're not always labeled. They can be used interchangeably but soft berries will cook quicker, which is why there is a large range for the cooking time. Begin checking on them early.

COOKING RIGHT

Finely chopped ginger will be just about the same size as the couscous, which means its flavor will permeate every bite.

COOKING AHEAD

To reheat, put the couscous in a heatproof serving dish, cover with foil, and put in a 350°F oven until heated through, about 15 minutes.

Couscous with Ginger, Orange, Almond & Herbs
SERVES 4 TO 6

Studded with flavor, this side dish will make a simple dinner special.

2 Tablespoons olive oil
½ medium yellow onion, finely chopped (about ½ cup)
1 clove garlic, finely chopped
2 Tablespoons finely minced fresh ginger
1 cup fresh orange juice (about 3 oranges), strained
1 Tablespoon unsalted butter
9 ounces (1½ cups) couscous
   Kosher salt and freshly ground black pepper
½ cup slivered almonds, toasted
¼ cup chopped fresh flat-leaf parsley
¼ cup chopped fresh cilantro
   Zest from 1 orange

In a large saucepan with a tight lid, heat the oil over medium heat. Add the onion and cook, stirring, until soft but not browned, 8 to 10 minutes. Stir in the garlic and ginger and cook for 2 minutes. Add the orange juice and cook until it has almost completely evaporated, about 10 minutes. Add 2 cups water and bring to a boil. Remove from the heat, stir in the butter, couscous, and 1 teaspoon of the salt. Cover and let stand for 15 minutes. With a fork, fluff the couscous. Stir in the almonds, parsley, cilantro, and orange zest and season with salt and pepper.

—EVA KATZ

Couscous with Cilantro & Melted Scallions

SERVES 6

This recipe can be put together in a matter of minutes and is wonderful with many dishes. It makes an attractive bed for kebabs; it pairs great with salmon, as shown here, but would also be delicious with the lamb brochettes on p. 130.

¼ cup unsalted butter
1 bunch scallions (whites and 2 inches of greens), minced (about ½ cup)
⅓ cup finely chopped fresh cilantro
10 ounces (1½ cups, or 1 box) couscous
3 cups homemade or low-salt canned chicken broth
　Kosher salt and freshly ground black pepper
　Juice of ½ lemon or lime

Melt the butter in a medium-sized saucepan over low heat, add the scallions, and cook, covered, until tender, about 8 minutes. Add the cilantro, couscous, broth, ¼ teaspoon salt, and pepper to taste. Stir, bring to a boil over high heat, cover, and remove from the heat. Set aside for 5 minutes. Fluff the couscous with a fork. Taste for salt, add a large grinding of pepper, and season with some of the lemon or lime juice.

—PERLA MEYERS

SIZING UP COUSCOUS

This recipe uses quick-cooking fine-grain couscous, which is probably what you'll find at the supermarket. But you can experiment with other styles and sizes of couscous, including medium-grain and Israeli. Just keep in mind that the larger the grain, the longer it will need to cook.

VEGETABLES

One of the many benefits of new American cooking has been a renewed respect for vegetables, with as much thought going into their preparation as the main course. The recipes here enhance old favorites—corn on the cob, glazed carrots, mashed potatoes—making them burst with flavor and excitement.

THE RECIPES

Seared Asparagus with Lemon & Parmesan Curls

Green Beans with Brown Butter & Pecans

Crispy Broccoli

Maple-Glazed Carrots

Baked Marinated Eggplant

Creamy Spinach

Sautéed Swiss Chard

Parmesan Puréed Potatoes

Smashed Red-Skinned Potatoes with Boursin & Scallions

Yukon Gold Gruyère Galette

Mustard & Rosemary Roasted Potatoes

Molasses Mashed Sweet Potatoes

Grilled Corn on the Cob with Lime-Cayenne Butter

Grilled Zucchini & Goat Cheese Roll-Ups

Zucchini & Summer Squash Gratin with Parmesan & Fresh Thyme

Red & Green Cabbage Salad with Cumin & Sherry Vinegar

Beets & Shallots with Crisp Prosciutto Dressing

Roasted Acorn Squash

Red Peppers Stuffed with Feta, Orzo, Lemon & Oregano

Fava Beans with Prosciutto, Mint & Garlic

Roasted Winter Vegetables

Braised Leeks & Mushrooms with Bacon, Lemon & Thyme

Browned Brussels Sprouts with Hazelnuts & Lemon

Seared Asparagus with Lemon & Parmesan Curls

SERVES 4 AS A SIDE DISH

Although you can choose to keep the spears whole in this dish, the asparagus will sear better if cut in half. Try serving them with the seared chicken breast on page 90.

¼ teaspoon grated lemon zest
1 teaspoon fresh lemon juice
2½ Tablespoons extra-virgin olive oil
1 pound large asparagus (about 16 spears), woody ends snapped off, spears peeled and cut in half crosswise
1 clove garlic, peeled and smashed
1 large shallot, cut into ¼-inch disks
  Pinch dried red chile flakes
  Kosher salt and freshly ground black pepper
¼ cup water; more if needed
10 shavings (2 inches long) Parmigiano Reggiano

COOKING RIGHT

For the best flavor, buy chunks of genuine Parmigiano Reggiano; the real stuff has its name stamped right on the rind. Use a vegetable peeler or cheese slicer to shave the cheese into curls.

Combine the lemon zest, lemon juice, and ½ tablespoon of the olive oil in a small bowl; set aside. Heat a heavy 12-inch skillet or large wok over high heat for 2 minutes. When the pan is hot, pour in the remaining 2 tablespoons olive oil, and a few seconds later, add the asparagus, garlic, shallot, and chile flakes. Season well with salt and pepper. Cook, shaking the pan often, until the asparagus begins to brown and starts to shrivel slightly, 3 to 4 minutes. Reduce the heat to medium low, carefully add the water (it will steam), and cover the pan with the lid ajar. Cook until the asparagus is just tender, 3 to 4 minutes. (If the water evaporates before the asparagus is done, add more, 1 tablespoon at a time.) Drizzle the lemon mixture over the asparagus. Season with salt and pepper. Transfer the asparagus to a small serving dish, top with the Parmesan curls, and serve immediately.

—TONY ROSENFELD

Green Beans with Brown Butter & Pecans

SERVES 8 TO 10

This toasty, buttery treatment can also transform Brussels sprouts; just cook them longer for a tender bite. Try either vegetable with the glazed chicken on p. 96.

- 2 pounds green beans, trimmed
- 8 Tablespoons (1 stick) butter, cut into pieces
- ¼ cup finely chopped shallots
- ½ cup chopped toasted pecans
- 2 Tablespoons fresh lemon juice
  Salt and freshly ground black pepper

Bring a large pot of salted water to a boil. Add the green beans; cook until tender, about 5 minutes. Plunge them into ice water to stop the cooking. Drain and reserve.

In a large skillet over medium-high heat, melt the butter. Add the shallots and pecans; cook, stirring, until the butter turns a light brown and begins to smell nutty (be careful not to burn it). Add the beans and toss to coat. Cook until the beans are warmed through, about 3 minutes. Add the lemon juice and season with salt and pepper.

—ROBERT CARTER

COOKING RIGHT

For faster trimming, gather a handful of beans, align their edges, and cut.

Crispy Broccoli

SERVES 4 AS A SIDE DISH

The fermented black beans are optional,
but they add a wonderful salty kick.
Look for them in Asian groceries.

1 Tablespoon soy sauce
1 teaspoon rice vinegar
1 teaspoon toasted sesame oil
3 Tablespoons peanut or canola oil
1 Tablespoon fermented black beans,
   rinsed, dried, and coarsely
   chopped (optional)
   Pinch dried red chile flakes
¾ pound broccoli crowns, cut into medium florets
¼ red bell pepper, finely diced
2 cloves garlic, peeled and smashed
1 piece (1 inch) fresh ginger, peeled and quartered
   Kosher salt
¼ cup water; more if needed

Combine the soy sauce, vinegar, sesame oil, and 1 tablespoon of the peanut oil in a small bowl; set aside. Heat a heavy 12-inch skillet or large wok over high heat for 2 minutes. When the pan is hot, pour in the remaining 2 tablespoons peanut oil; a couple of seconds later, add the black beans (if using), the chile flakes, broccoli, red pepper, garlic, and ginger. Season the mixture well with salt and cook, tossing or stirring often, until the broccoli deepens to a dark green and browns in places, 3 to 4 minutes. Reduce the heat to medium low, carefully add the water (it will steam), and cover the pan with the lid ajar. Cook until the broccoli softens but still has some crunch, about 4 minutes. (If the water evaporates before the broccoli is done, add more, 1 tablespoon at a time.) Stir the soy sauce mixture well and drizzle it over the broccoli, toss well, and serve immediately.

—TONY ROSENFELD

COOKING RIGHT

Sear for flavor. High heat caramelizes the broccoli, giving it a sweet, intense flavor.

Steam for texture. Water loosens up the flavorful browned bits on the bottom of the pan and steams the vegetables till tender but still crisp.

Maple-Glazed Carrots

SERVES 4 TO 6

These are delicious with roast pork and cornbread. Pure maple syrup is essential.

1½ pounds carrots (about 8), peeled and trimmed
   About 1 cup water
2 Tablespoons unsalted butter
1½ Tablespoons pure maple syrup
1 teaspoon kosher salt; more as needed

Cut the carrots using a roll cut as described below. (Or substitute another cut as long as the pieces are close to equal in size, or use baby carrots.)

Put the carrots in a large sauté pan (they should be almost in a single layer) and add enough water to come halfway up the sides of the carrots. Add the butter, maple syrup, and salt and bring to a boil over high heat. Cover the pan with the lid slightly askew, reduce the heat to medium-high, and cook at a steady boil, shaking the pan occasionally, until the carrots are tender but not soft (a paring knife should enter the carrot with just a little resistance), about 10 minutes. Uncover and continue to boil until the liquid evaporates and forms a syrup and the carrots become lightly tinged with brown. Shake the pan and roll the pieces around to evenly glaze the carrots. Taste and add a pinch of salt, if needed, and serve.

—TASHA PRYSI

CUTTING CARROTS

For a pretty presentation, try a roll cut. Begin by trimming the carrot tip with a sharp diagonal cut. Roll the carrot 180 degrees and cut off a 1-inch piece, keeping your knife at the same diagonal as the original cut. Continue to roll and cut the carrot in this way. If the carrot widens dramatically, adjust the knife angle and carrot length so all the pieces are the same size.

Which eggplant is which? From top to bottom: American, Italian, Chinese, Japanese

Baked Marinated Eggplant
SERVES 6 TO 8 AS PART OF AN ANTIPASTO

If you can't find Italian eggplant, the Japanese variety is a good alternative. Like the Italian, it has dense flesh with fewer seeds and less water than the globe variety.

1½ pounds Italian eggplant
¼ cup olive oil
    Salt and freshly ground black pepper
2 Tablespoons finely diced red onion
2 Tablespoons red-wine vinegar
4 Tablespoons extra-virgin olive oil
1 Tablespoon chopped fresh mint

Heat the oven to 375°F. Cut away the eggplant stem, and cut the eggplant lengthwise into ¼-inch slices. Brush the slices on both sides with olive oil and sprinkle them with salt and pepper.

Pour enough water into two sheet pans to just cover the bottoms. Arrange the eggplant slices side by side on each pan. Cover with foil and bake for 25 minutes. Remove the foil and bake until the eggplant has dried somewhat, 15 to 20 minutes. Take care during the second stage of the cooking to remove the eggplant before it sticks to the pan.

Transfer the cooked eggplant to a large serving platter. In a small bowl, combine the red onion and vinegar. Add a pinch of salt and pepper. Stir to dissolve the salt. Stir in the extra-virgin olive oil and mint. While the eggplant is still warm, spoon a little of the vinaigrette over each slice. Let stand for 30 minutes. Serve the eggplant at room temperature as part of an antipasto.

—PAUL BERTOLLI

Creamy Spinach

SERVES 4

This is lighter-than-traditional creamed spinach. You can turn it into a spinach gratin by pouring on a little additional cream, topping with a mixture of grated Parmesan and Gruyère, and baking until browned and bubbling.

3 bunches spinach (10 to 12 ounces each), trimmed and well washed
2 Tablespoons unsalted butter
¼ cup minced scallions (white and light green parts)
¾ cup heavy cream
   Kosher salt and freshly ground black pepper

Bring a large pot of salted water to a boil. Add the spinach and boil it until it wilts completely, about 1 minute. Drain in a colander and cool the spinach under cold running water. Squeeze the spinach with your hands to remove excess water. Chop the spinach coarsely and set it aside. In a large skillet over medium heat, melt the butter. Add the scallions and cook for 2 minutes, stirring occasionally. Add the spinach, the cream, and ½ teaspoon of salt. Raise the heat to medium high. Cook, breaking up the spinach with a wooden spoon, until the spinach is tender and has absorbed most of the cream and the pan is still a bit saucy, 3 to 5 minutes. Remove from the heat, season with black pepper and additional salt as needed, and serve.

—ALAN TANGREN

Bunched spinach is easy to trim with one quick pass of the knife.

Tough ribs, found in all but the youngest spinach, must go. Gently fold the leaf over and pull the stem and rib off as if stringing a bean.

COOKING RIGHT

Before sautéing, the thick part of the Swiss chard's stem needs to be removed with a knife. The leaves then get split in half, following the line of the center rib, and are cut into smaller pieces.

Sautéed Swiss Chard

SERVES 4

Swiss chard is a lot like spinach, only sturdier. Try it alongside roast lamb or braised short ribs, such as the ones on p.113. Once you've tried this basic recipe, experiment with the flavorings shown on the facing page.

2 pounds Swiss chard (about 2 bunches)
2 Tablespoons extra-virgin olive oil
2 teaspoons finely chopped garlic (about 4 cloves)
   Kosher salt
   Pinch crushed red chile flakes

Fill a sink with cold water and wash the Swiss chard to remove any grit. Transfer to paper towels and let dry for a couple of minutes (it's fine if a little water clings to the leaves).

Remove the thick part of each stem by cutting a V-shaped notch partway into the leaf. Split each leaf in half lengthwise by slicing down the center rib. Stack the halved leaves (in batches if necessary) and cut them in half crosswise to get 4- to 6-inch pieces.

Heat the oil in a large skillet over medium-high heat for 1 minute. Working in batches, pile the Swiss chard into the pan, turning and tossing gently until the leaves begin to wilt and turn glossy. Add a new batch of leaves as the previous batch wilts and makes room for more.

When all the chard is wilted, sprinkle in the garlic and a little salt and toss well. Lower the heat to medium low, cover, and cook for 4 minutes. Remove the lid, raise the heat to high, add the chile flakes, and continue to cook for 2 minutes so that much of the liquid evaporates; the leaves should be tender but not overly soft. Serve immediately.

—ARLENE JACOBS

Slivered Almonds & Browned Butter

2 Tablespoons unsalted butter
⅓ cup slivered almonds
1 teaspoon fresh lemon juice
2 Tablespoons finely chopped shallots

In a small sauté pan or saucepan, melt the butter over medium heat. Add the almonds, reduce the heat to medium low, and cook, stirring often, until the nuts are golden and the milk solids in the butter turn a nutty brown. Remove from the heat and stir in the lemon juice. Keep warm.

Make the basic sautéed Swiss chard, replacing the garlic in the recipe with the shallots. Sprinkle the almonds and butter over the finished chard and serve immediately.

Sun-Dried Tomatoes & Feta

6 oil-packed sun-dried tomato halves, drained and cut into thin strips
⅓ cup feta, crumbled
½ teaspoon lightly chopped fresh thyme leaves

Combine the sun-dried tomatoes, feta, and thyme in a bowl. Make the basic sautéed Swiss chard, add the feta mixture at the end, toss, and serve immediately.

Asian-Style with Ginger & Peanuts

1 Tablespoon minced fresh ginger
½ red bell pepper, cut into very thin strips
1 teaspoon sugar
¼ cup unsalted roasted shelled peanuts, coarsely chopped

Make the basic sautéed Swiss chard, but add the ginger, red bell pepper, and sugar at the same time as the garlic. At the end, sprinkle with the peanuts and serve immediately.

Gremolata (Lemon-Garlic)

2 teaspoons finely grated lemon zest (about 1 lemon)
1 small clove garlic, very finely chopped
2 Tablespoons minced fresh flat-leaf parsley

Combine the lemon zest, garlic, and parsley in a bowl. Make the basic sautéed Swiss chard, add the mixture (called gremolata) at the end, toss, and serve immediately.

Anchovies, Parmesan & Breadcrumbs

6 anchovy fillets, drained and minced
⅓ cup freshly grated Parmigiano Reggiano
½ cup fresh breadcrumbs, toasted

Make the basic sautéed Swiss chard. Add the anchovies and Parmigiano at the end and toss. Sprinkle with the toasted breadcrumbs and serve immediately.

Parmesan Puréed Potatoes

SERVES 8 TO 10

Be sure you're using actual Parmigiano Reggiano for this dish. (It must be labeled as such.) An inferior cheese won't give you the nutty, round flavor you're after.

3½ to 4 pounds medium-starch
    potatoes, preferably Yukon Golds, peeled, quartered, and rinsed
  2 teaspoons kosher salt
1½ cups milk; more if needed
  ½ cup heavy cream
  8 Tablespoons (1 stick) unsalted butter, at room temperature
  ½ cup freshly grated Parmigiano Reggiano
    Freshly ground black pepper

Put the quartered potatoes in a large saucepan with enough cold water to cover. Partially cover the pot and bring to a boil. Uncover, add the salt, and reduce the heat so the water boils gently. Cook until the potatoes are tender when pierced with a fork, 10 to 12 minutes. Meanwhile, heat the milk and cream on the stovetop or in a microwave until hot but not boiling. Drain the potatoes and return to the warm pan over low heat for 1 minute, shaking the pan to dry the potatoes thoroughly. Use a potato masher, a ricer, or a food mill to mash the potatoes. Blend the butter and Parmigiano into the potatoes. Gradually add the milk mixture until the purée is as soft and moist as you like. Add salt and pepper to taste and serve.

—DIANE MORGAN

COOK'S CHOICE

If you can find it, try substituting Gorgonzola dolce, which is soft and yellow with greenish-blue lines, for the boursin.

Smashed Red-Skinned Potatoes with Boursin & Scallions

SERVES 4 TO 6

Smashing low-starch potatoes into a rustic side dish is the way to go to avoid gumminess. Besides, there is always someone who loves lumps.

1¾ to 2 pounds red-skinned potatoes, scrubbed and cut into 1½- to 2-inch chunks
　　Kosher salt

2 Tablespoons unsalted butter, cut into pieces and softened

4 ounces boursin (with garlic and herbs), cut into pieces and at room temperature

3 scallions (white parts with some green), chopped
　　Freshly ground black pepper

Put the potatoes in a large saucepan and cover with cold water by at least an inch. Add a generous ½ teaspoon salt and bring to a boil. Lower the heat to maintain a steady simmer, cover the pot partially, and cook until the potatoes are quite tender when tested with a metal skewer, 15 to 20 minutes.

Drain the potatoes—reserving some of the cooking water—and dump them back in the pot. Dry the potatoes over medium heat, shaking the pan and stirring, until most of the moisture has steamed off. Reduce the heat to very low.

Use the side of a big metal spoon to cut through the skins and flesh of the potatoes, reducing the chunks to a very coarse mash. Stir in the butter and then the boursin. You might need to loosen the mash with a few tablespoons cooking water or as much as ½ cup. Don't beat vigorously or the potatoes may turn gummy. Stir in the scallions, add salt and pepper, and serve right away.

　　　　　　　　　　　　—ROY FINAMORE AND MOLLY STEVENS

COOKING RIGHT

A big metal spoon is the best tool for making smashed potatoes where you want to retain texture and lumps.

COOK'S CHOICE

Make tiny tarts. Use four 4½-inch tart pans with removable bottoms and bake for just a little less time. If baking ahead, remove them from the tart pan and reheat on a baking sheet.

Yukon Gold Gruyère Galette

SERVES 4 TO 6 AS A SIDE DISH

A wedge of galette makes a lovely bed for beef tenderloin or a pot-roasted pork served with a little sauce, such as the one on p. 122.

¼ cup finely chopped shallots (about 2 large shallots)

3 Tablespoons extra-virgin olive oil plus ½ teaspoon for the pan (or use olive-oil spray for the pan)

1 pound Yukon Gold potatoes (about 2 large or 3 medium), unpeeled and scrubbed

1 heaping teaspoon very lightly chopped fresh thyme
Kosher salt

½ cup finely grated Parmigiano Reggiano (about a 1½-ounce piece, grated on a box grater's small holes)

1 cup finely grated Gruyère (about 3½ ounces)

Combine the shallots and 3 table-spoons of the oil in a small saucepan and bring to a simmer over medium heat. Reduce to a low simmer; cook the shallots until nicely softened (don't let them brown), about 2 minutes. Remove from the heat and let cool completely (about 25 minutes at room temperature; cool them more quickly in the refrigerator, if you like).

Heat the oven to 400°F. Rub the bottom and inside edge of a 7½-inch tart pan with a removable bottom with the remaining ½ teaspoon olive oil or spray with olive-oil spray. Put the tart pan on a rimmed baking sheet lined with foil.

COOKING AHEAD

Cut the galette into wedges before reheating. (Wedges can go right from the oven to the plate; a whole galette would need to cool a bit before slicing.) Heat the wedges on a baking sheet at 350°F for about 15 minutes.

Slice the potatoes as thinly as possible (about 1⁄16 inch) with a chef's knife. Tip: If the potato wobbles, slice a thin lengthwise sliver off the bottom to stabilize it; then continue slicing crosswise. Discard the ends. Put the potato slices in a mixing bowl, add the shallots and olive oil along with the thyme and toss well to thoroughly coat the potatoes (a small rubber spatula works well).

Cover the bottom of the tart pan with a layer of potato slices, overlapping them slightly. Start along the outside edge of the tart pan and, making slightly overlapping rings, move inward until the bottom is covered with one layer of potatoes. Sprinkle the potatoes with salt (a generous 1⁄8 teaspoon) and then sprinkle about one quarter of the Parmigiano and about one quarter of the Gruyère over all. Arrange another layer of potatoes, season with salt, sprinkle with cheese, and repeat two more times, until you have four layers of potatoes. (The last layer will mound up a bit higher than the edge of the pan.) Top the last layer with more salt and any remaining cheese.

Bake the galette until the top is a reddish golden brown and the potatoes are tender in all places (a fork with thin tines should poke easily through all the layers), 45 to 50 minutes. The bottom will be crisp and the sides brown.

Let the galette cool for 10 or 15 minutes in the pan. It will then be cool enough to handle but still plenty hot inside for serving. Have a cutting board nearby. Run a paring knife around the edge of the galette to loosen it and carefully remove the tart ring by gently pressing the tart bottom up. Slide a very thin spatula under and all around the bottom layer to free the galette from the tart bottom. Use the spatula to gently slide the galette onto a cutting board. Cut into four or six wedges, or as many as you like.

—SUSIE MIDDLETON

COOKING RIGHT

Start layering the potatoes on the outside of the pan and work inward. Sprinkle the first layer with cheese before arranging the next layer of potatoes.

COOKING AHEAD

After roasting, the potatoes can be held, loosely covered, in a low (200°F) oven for up to an hour before serving, which makes them great for entertaining.

Mustard & Rosemary Roasted Potatoes

SERVES 4 TO 6

These potatoes start out looking very wet, but the mixture cooks down to leave the potatoes crisp, crusty, and tangy.

⅓ cup plus 1 Tablespoon Dijon mustard

¼ cup olive oil

1 Tablespoon dry vermouth or other dry white wine

2 cloves garlic, minced

1 Tablespoon chopped fresh rosemary

1 teaspoon coarse salt
    Freshly ground black pepper

2 pounds red-skinned potatoes, cut into ¾- to 1-inch dice

Heat the oven to 400°F. In a large mixing bowl, whisk together the mustard, olive oil, vermouth, garlic, rosemary, salt, and pepper. Add the potatoes and toss to coat. Dump the potatoes onto a large, rimmed baking sheet and spread them in a single layer. Roast, tossing with a spatula a few times, until the potatoes are crusty on the outside and tender throughout, 50 to 55 minutes. Serve hot.

—MOLLY STEVENS

The mustard mix will look gloppy at first. Just keep tossing until the potatoes are evenly coated.

Molasses Mashed Sweet Potatoes

SERVES 4

This mash is a great partner for pork, duck, and all kinds of game; the small amount of molasses really deepens the flavor but doesn't become cloying.

2   medium sweet potatoes
    (1 pound total), peeled and
    cut into 1-inch chunks
4   small carrots (½ pound total), peeled and cut into 1-inch chunks
2   medium parsnips (½ pound total), peeled and cut into 1-inch chunks
    Salt
2   Tablespoons unsalted butter
2   Tablespoons sour cream
2   Tablespoons molasses
2   teaspoons grated fresh ginger
¼   cup half-and-half
    Freshly ground black pepper

In a large saucepan, combine the sweet potatoes, carrots, and parsnips; cover with cold water. Bring to a boil, add a dash of salt, and simmer until tender, 15 to 20 minutes. Drain and return to the saucepan. Set the pan over low heat, uncovered, and let the vegetables dry in the pan for about 2 minutes, shaking the pan occasionally so they don't stick. Pass the vegetables through a food mill or mash them by hand, if you prefer. Stir in the butter, sour cream, molasses, grated ginger, and half-and-half. (If you're preparing the potatoes ahead, save 2 tablespoons of the half-and-half for reheating.) Add ½ teaspoon salt and pepper, adjust the seasonings, and serve.

—KAREN AND BEN BARKER

Use a masher to give the potatoes a rustic texture. . .

. . . or put them through a food mill for smoother results.

COOKING AHEAD

You can make this up to a day ahead and then reheat it before serving.

Grilled Corn on the Cob with Lime-Cayenne Butter

MAKES 8 TO 10 EARS OF CORN

The tart and spicy butter really brings out the sweet, smoky flavors of the grilled corn. You'll get the best smoky flavor with a grill fueled by hardwood charcoal, but a gas grill will certainly cook the kernels.

8   Tablespoons (1 stick) unsalted butter
    Juice of 1 lime
1   teaspoon coarse salt
½   teaspoon cayenne
8   to 10 ears of corn

Melt the butter in a small saucepan and stir in the lime juice, salt, and cayenne. Keep warm.

Remove the outer layers of the husk but leave a couple layers on the kernels. Light a charcoal grill. When the coals are red-hot, put the corn on and cook, turning often, until the first layer of husk is completely charred, 5 to 10 minutes. Transfer to a platter and keep warm. Just before serving, pull off the charred husks, brush off any burnt silks, and put the corn back on the grill for a minute to brown the kernels a bit. Brush the lime-cayenne butter lavishly on hot grilled corn and serve immediately.

—LISA HANAUE

GRILLED CORN ADDS A SMOKY ACCENT

Leftover (unbuttered) grilled corn can be used in many delicious ways. Simply remove the kernels as shown at left, store them in an airtight container, and use them the next day in one of the following ways:

- Fold grilled corn into soft polenta.

- Scatter grilled corn over a ripe tomato salad.

- Fold grilled corn, crisped pancetta, and snipped chives into an omelet.

- Add grilled corn to your favorite salsas.

- Add grilled corn to a favorite vegetable pasta.

Grilled Zucchini & Goat Cheese Roll-Ups

YIELDS 8 TO 10 ROLL-UPS

Make these ahead, refrigerate them if you like, and broil them briefly before serving. Serve with a first-course green salad or as a side to grilled meat, or as part of an antipasto.

- 3 small zucchini, cut lengthwise into ¼-inch-thick strips
  Olive oil
- 3 ounces goat cheese, at room temperature
- ⅛ teaspoon kosher salt
- 1 Tablespoon finely chopped oil-packed sun-dried tomatoes, well drained
  Heaping ½ teaspoon fresh thyme, chopped
- 2 Tablespoons freshly grated Parmigiano Reggiano

COOKING RIGHT

To slice zucchini for roll-ups, trim off both ends. Then even the rounded long sides by trimming just a little bit off. Cut the remainder lengthwise.

Heat a gas grill to high. Brush both sides of the zucchini with olive oil and grill with the grill cover down, until browned and limp, 3 to 4 minutes per side. Transfer the grilled zucchini to a cooling rack to keep them from steaming as they cool.

In a bowl, combine the goat cheese, salt, sun-dried tomatoes, oil, and thyme. Spread 1 heaping teaspoon of the filling thinly over one side of each grilled zucchini strip (use a mini spatula or your fingers to spread). Roll up the zucchini (not too tightly; this is more like folding), and put them on a baking sheet lined with parchment or foil. Refrigerate if not using within an hour, but bring back to room temperature before broiling. Heat the broiler. Sprinkle with a little grated Parmigiano and brown under the broiler, about 1 minute.

—SUSIE MIDDLETON

COOKING AHEAD

You can fully cook the gratin hours ahead, let it cool, and reheat it again before serving. Its flavors will only be more intense.

Cut the vegetables on the bias to increase the size of slices from small squash.

Alternate the rows of vegetables for a striking effect. Sprinkle the cheese between the rows and give the rows an occasional gentle push to help compact them.

Zucchini & Summer Squash Gratin with Parmesan & Fresh Thyme

SERVES 6 TO 8 AS A SIDE DISH

For this gratin, use all the interesting green and yellow summer squashes (pattypan, scallop, crookneck, butterstick) you find at the farmers' market.

For the onions:

- 2 Tablespoons olive oil
- 2 medium onions (14 ounces total), thinly sliced

For the gratin:

- 1¼ pounds small ripe tomatoes, cored and cut into ¼-inch slices
- ¾ pound (about 2 small) zucchini or other green summer squash, cut into ¼-inch slices on the bias
- ¾ pound (about 2 small) yellow summer squash or golden zucchini, cut into ¼-inch slices on the bias
- 3 Tablespoons olive oil
- ¼ cup fresh thyme leaves
- 1 teaspoon coarse salt
- 1¼ cups freshly grated Parmigiano Reggiano
  Freshly ground black pepper

Cook the onions—Heat the olive oil in a medium skillet over medium heat. Add the onions and cook, stirring, until limp and golden brown, about 20 minutes. Spread the onions evenly in the bottom of an oiled 2-quart shallow gratin dish (preferably oval). Let cool.

Assemble the gratin—Heat the oven to 375°F. Put the tomato slices on a shallow plate to drain for a few minutes and then discard the collected juices. In a medium bowl, toss the zucchini and squash slices with 1½ tablespoons of the olive oil, 2 tablespoons of the thyme, and ½ teaspoon of the salt. Reserve half of the cheese for the top of the gratin.

Sprinkle 1 tablespoon of the thyme over the onions in the gratin. Starting at one end of the baking dish, lay a row of slightly overlapping tomato slices across the width of the dish and sprinkle with a little of the cheese. Next, lay a row of zucchini, overlapping the tomatoes by two-thirds, and sprinkle with cheese. Repeat with a row of squash, and then repeat rows, sprinkling each with cheese, until the gratin is full.

Season lightly with pepper and the remaining ½ teaspoon salt. Drizzle the remaining 1½ tablespoons olive oil over all. Combine the reserved cheese with the remaining 1 tablespoon thyme and sprinkle this over the whole gratin. Cook until well-browned all over and the juices have bubbled for a while and reduced considerably, 65 to 70 minutes. Let cool for at least 15 minutes before serving.

—SUSIE MIDDLETON

COOKING RIGHT

Let the onions get good and brown; they add a layer of deep flavor to the dish.

COOKING AHEAD

The components of the salad can all be prepared hours ahead and mixed at the last minute.

Red & Green Cabbage Salad with Cumin & Sherry Vinegar

SERVES 6 TO 8

Heated vinegar softens the cabbage's texture and helps the flavors penetrate. This is wonderful alongside pork chops.

½ head green cabbage, cored and cut in thin strips
½ head red cabbage, cored and cut in thin strips
6 Tablespoons sherry vinegar
½ teaspoon cumin seeds
   Salt and freshly ground black pepper
4 thick slices bacon, cooked until crisp and crumbled
1 small carrot, peeled and finely diced
1 apple, peeled and finely diced
3 Tablespoons finely chopped flat-leaf parsley
3 Tablespoons walnut pieces, lightly toasted in a dry skillet
1 Tablespoon sugar
2 Tablespoons olive oil

COOKING RIGHT

To core cabbage, cut it in half first and use a knife to cut out its tough, triangular core.

Bring a large pot of water to a boil. Fill a large bowl with ice water. Add the green cabbage to the boiling water and blanch it for 1 minute. With a slotted spoon, transfer the cabbage to the ice water to halt the cooking. Drain the cabbage well and set aside in another bowl. Repeat with the red cabbage. Set the red cabbage aside in a second bowl (so its color doesn't bleed into the green cabbage).

In a small saucepan, bring the vinegar to a boil. Pour half the vinegar over the green cabbage and toss well; repeat with the red cabbage. Divide the cumin seeds between the two bowls of cabbage; season both with salt and pepper. Let the cabbage marinate about 20 minutes.

Drain the cabbages separately, put them in a large mixing bowl, and toss. Add the bacon, carrot, apple, parsley, toasted walnuts, sugar, and olive oil. Toss several times, taste for seasoning, and add salt, pepper, or vinegar if needed.

—HUBERT KELLER

Beets & Shallots
with Crisp Prosciutto Dressing
SERVES 4

These are great on top of crisp greens
or served as a colorful side to a rib-eye steak.

1   pound small or medium red or yellow beets,
    scrubbed but not peeled, cut into wedges
    1½ inches across at their widest
5   large shallots, peeled and halved through the stem
    Extra-virgin olive oil
    Kosher salt
5   small sprigs fresh thyme or rosemary
2   ounces thinly sliced prosciutto, cut into thin strips
1   clove garlic, thinly sliced
1½ Tablespoons sherry vinegar
    Pinch dried red chile flakes
15 large mint leaves, thinly sliced (1 heaping tablespoon)

Heat the oven to 400°F. Measure two 2-foot lengths of aluminum foil
and crisscross them on a small, rimmed baking sheet. Toss the beets and
shallots with about 1 tablespoon of olive oil and season with ½ teaspoon
of salt. Put them, in one snug layer, on the cross section of foil. Lay the
herb sprigs on top. Fold each layer of foil in and seal to create a tight,
flat, and relatively airtight package. Roast the beets until done (a thin
knife should slide through without resistance), about 1½ hours.

Heat 2 tablespoons of olive oil in a medium skillet over medium- high heat.
Add the prosciutto and sauté until crisp, 2 to 3 minutes; transfer with a
slotted spoon to paper towels. Turn the heat down to medium low, add
the garlic and sauté until barely turning golden, 30 to 60 seconds. Add
the vinegar, a big pinch of salt, and a few red chile flakes. Stir and remove
the pan from the heat. Toss the warm beets and shallots with the warm
dressing. Reserving a little of each for garnish, toss the mint and prosciutto
into the pan with the beets and stir again. Turn the beets out onto a
small platter and top with the remaining mint and prosciutto.

—SUSIE MIDDLETON

COOKING AHEAD

You can roast the beets and shallots a day ahead of dressing them.
Spread the roasted vegetables on a
foil-lined baking sheet and heat for
10 minutes in a 350°F oven; they
just need to be warm, not piping hot.

COOKING RIGHT

Wrapping the beats in foil creates
steam, which helps the beet wedges
cook faster yet they will still cara-
melize on the bottom where they are
in contact with a hot pan.

Roasted Acorn Squash

EACH SQUASH YIELDS 2 SUBSTANTIAL SIDE-DISH SERVINGS

Choose acorn squash on the smaller side; they'll be more tender and will cook more quickly.

1 acorn squash (about 1¼ pounds)
¼ teaspoon coarse salt
1½ Tablespoons unsalted butter, softened
1½ Tablespoons brown sugar

Heat the oven to 400°F. Slice a thin piece off both ends of the squash, including the stem. Cut the squash in half crosswise (perpendicular to the ribs). Scoop out the seeds with a sturdy spoon.

Line a rimmed baking sheet, jellyroll pan, or shallow baking dish with foil or parchment. (If you're only cooking two halves, be sure to use a small pan that the squash will fit into somewhat snugly.) If you use foil, rub it with butter to keep the squash from sticking.

Set the squash halves on the prepared baking sheet and smear the flesh all over with the softened butter. Sprinkle with the salt. Sprinkle or drizzle the brown sugar (or other flavoring) over the top edge of the squash and into the cavity (most of the liquid will pool up there).

Roast the squash halves until nicely browned and very tender (poke in several places with a fork to test), about 1 hour and 15 minutes for small to medium squash; larger squash may take longer. Don't undercook. Serve warm with a spoon.

—SUSIE MIDDLETON

COOK'S CHOICE

In place of the brown sugar, try one of the following flavors:

Apple Cider: 2 tablespoons apple cider mixed with 1 tablespoon honey and a pinch of brown sugar

Orange-Curry: 2 tablespoons orange juice mixed with 1 tablespoon honey, 1 teaspoon fresh ginger, and a pinch of curry powder

Maple-Pecan: 2 tablespoons maple syrup (Add 2 tablespoons chopped pecans during the last 10 minutes of cooking.)

Red Peppers Stuffed with Feta, Orzo, Lemon & Oregano

YIELDS 4 PEPPERS

Cooking the peppers uncovered gives them a delicious, slightly roasted flavor. Serve them with a little of the pan juices spooned over them.

4	Tablespoons olive oil
1	medium red onion, cut into large dice
2½	ounces kale, washed and torn into bite-size pieces (2 cups lightly packed)
	Salt and freshly ground black pepper
1⅔	cups cooked orzo, cooled (¾ cup raw orzo)
	Grated zest from ½ lemon
1	to 2 Tablespoons fresh lemon juice (about ½ lemon)
¼	pound feta
1	teaspoon chopped fresh oregano or ½ teaspoon dried
1½	teaspoons chopped fresh thyme
1	Tablespoon chopped fresh flat-leaf parsley
8	kalamata olives, pitted and chopped
4	medium red bell peppers, preferably Holland peppers
1½	cups dry white wine or water

COOKING RIGHT

Pick a pretty pepper. Holland peppers, with their even size and shape, look great and will stand up in the pan. If they do wobble, trim a tiny bit from the bottom to even the base.

Heat the oven to 350°F. Heat 2 tablespoons of the oil in a large skillet until moderately hot. Add the red onion and cook, stirring, until soft, about 5 minutes. Add the kale and cook, stirring often, until tender, 5 to 7 minutes. Season with a little salt and pepper and reserve.

In a medium bowl, combine the onion and kale with the orzo, lemon zest, lemon juice, feta, oregano, thyme, parsley, and olives. Toss gently until combined and season with salt and pepper.

Slice off the top ½ inch of each pepper and reserve. With a paring knife, cut away the ribs. Pat out the seeds. Divide the filling among the peppers and replace the top. Put the peppers in a baking dish and sprinkle them with the remaining 2 tablespoons olive oil, salt, and pepper. Pour the wine in the pan. Bake until very tender and slightly blackened on top, about 1½ hours.

—GORDON HAMERSLEY

Fava Beans with Prosciutto, Mint & Garlic

SERVES 2 AS A SIDE DISH

A pound and a half of fava bean pods will only yield a scant cup of beans, so this recipe is designed to serve two people. If you want to double the recipe, you can use shelled fresh peas in place of the extra cup of favas if you like. The beans are delicious with grilled shrimp.

1½ pounds fresh fava beans in the pod, shelled
 2 Tablespoons extra-virgin olive oil
 2 Tablespoons minced prosciutto
 1 teaspoon minced garlic
 ½ teaspoon coarse salt
 ½ teaspoon balsamic vinegar
 8 large mint leaves, finely chopped (2 to 3 teaspoons)

Peel the shelled beans by boiling them for a couple of minutes to loosen the skin around the bean just enough for you to pinch it off (see the photo at left).

In a medium-sized skillet, heat the olive oil over medium heat. Add the prosciutto and sauté for 1 minute. Add the garlic and sauté, stirring constantly, until it's very fragrant and just beginning to turn brown, another 1 to 2 minutes. Add the fava beans, season with the salt, and sauté until the favas are heated and coated well with the pan contents, another 2 minutes. (Some of the beans will begin to turn a lighter color.) Add the balsamic vinegar, turn off the heat, and stir to coat. Add the mint and stir to combine and wilt it. Taste for salt; depending on the saltiness of your prosciutto, you might want to add more.

—SUSIE MIDDLETON

COOKING RIGHT

To slip the skin off a fava bean, pinch one end of the parboiled bean with a thumbnail, squeeze, and out it pops.

COOK'S CHOICE

Domestic prosciutto works just fine in this dish, but imported versions of this thin-sliced Italian ham, such as prosciutto di Parma, make the dish taste even better.

Roasted Winter Vegetables

SERVES 4

Rosemary's pine flavor complements the natural sweetness of sweet potatoes and parsnips.

 2 medium carrots (about 8 ounces), peeled and cut into ¾-inch chunks
 1 medium onion, cut into 1-inch pieces
 1 medium sweet potato (about 8 ounces), peeled and cut into
     1-inch cubes
 8 ounces mixed mushrooms, cut (if necessary) into 1-inch pieces
 2 medium parsnips (about 8 ounces), peeled and cut into 1-inch cubes
10 garlic cloves, peeled
 3 Tablespoons extra-virgin olive oil
 1 Tablespoon balsamic vinegar
 2 teaspoons coarse salt
 1 Tablespoon chopped fresh rosemary
     Chopped fresh parsley for garnish

Heat the oven to 450°F. In a large bowl, toss the carrots, onion, sweet potato, mushrooms, parsnips, and garlic with the olive oil, balsamic vinegar, salt, and rosemary. Spread the vegetables out in a baking pan just large enough to hold them in one layer. Roast, shaking the pan once or twice, until the vegetables are a toasty caramel color and fork tender, about 50 minutes. Garnish with chopped fresh parsley and serve hot or at room temperature.

—LUCIA WATSON AND BETH DOOLEY

ROAST VEGETABLES FOR EVERY SEASON

Use this technique to roast just about any combination of vegetables and flavorings, adjusting the timing as needed.

- asparagus and mushrooms with walnut oil and tarragon vinegar

- corn and peas with olive oil, basil, and mint

- red onions with olive oil and sherry vinegar

- butternut squash with hazelnut oil

- zucchini, fennel, and tomatoes with olive oil and parsley

COOKING RIGHT

Use your hands to toss the vegetables to evenly distribute the salt and seasonings.

Braised Leeks & Mushrooms with Bacon, Lemon & Thyme

SERVES 4

Try this adaptable side dish alongside beef, chicken, or even a hearty seafood like monkfish.

COOKING RIGHT

Use high heat for the best flavor.
Let the mushrooms cook, undisturbed, until well browned on one side. Then stir them occasionally until their juices have released and evaporated and they are well browned on all sides.

¾ cup chopped bacon (3 large slices)
2 cups thinly sliced leeks, white and light green parts only (2 medium), rinsed well and dried
4 cups (about 1 pound) mixed mushrooms, large caps quartered, small caps left whole
¼ teaspoon coarse salt
2 teaspoons grated lemon zest
1 Tablespoon fresh thyme leaves
  Freshly ground black pepper
¾ cup homemade or low-salt canned chicken or vegetable stock

Put the bacon in a large skillet and set the skillet over medium heat. Cook until the bacon has begun to crisp and is half-cooked, about 8 minutes.

Add the leeks and increase the heat to medium high. Cook, stirring frequently, until the leeks are soft (the bacon will continue to crisp), about 6 minutes. Using a slotted spoon or skimmer, transfer the bacon and leeks to a bowl, leaving the fat in the pan.

Add the mushrooms to the pan and cook quickly, stirring occasionally, until the mushrooms are browned, about 6 minutes. Add the salt, lemon zest, thyme, and the leek and bacon mixture. Add pepper generously (about 10 grinds) and stir.

Add the stock to the pan and bring to a boil, stirring to scrape the bottom of the pan. Cover the pan and reduce the heat to medium low. Braise slowly until the mushrooms are very tender and the liquid is absorbed, about 20 minutes. If the mushrooms are tender but still brothy, raise the heat and boil, uncovered, until the broth has reduced considerably. Taste a mushroom and add more salt and pepper if needed.

—SUSAN GOSS

Browned Brussels Sprouts with Hazelnuts & Lemon

YIELDS 4 CUPS; SERVES 8

This nutty, buttery take on Brussels sprouts is sure to win over even those who say they don't like them. Serve these with roast chicken.

½ cup hazelnuts
2 Tablespoons olive oil
2 Tablespoons unsalted butter
2 pounds fresh Brussels sprouts,
   trimmed and quartered
   Kosher salt
2 to 4 Tablespoons fresh lemon juice
   Freshly ground black pepper

Toast the nuts on a baking sheet in a 350°F oven, stirring occasionally, until very fragrant and the skins are deep brown and cracked, about 15 minutes. Wrap the nuts in a clean dishtowel (one you don't mind staining); let steam for at least 5 minutes. Vigorously rub the nuts against one another in the towel to scrape off the skins (you won't get them all; aim for about half). Chop the nuts coarsely.

Heat a 12-inch skillet over medium-high heat. When the pan is hot, add the oil and butter. As soon as the butter melts, add the Brussels sprouts and spread evenly around the pan. Sprinkle with salt and cook without disturbing until browned on the first side, about 3 minutes. Continue to cook, stirring the sprouts occasionally, until they're well browned all over, another 5 to 8 minutes. Add ¼ cup water, cover partially, and cook until tender, another 4 to 5 minutes (if the water evaporates completely during cooking, add more, 2 tablespoons at a time). Don't over-cook; the sprouts shouldn't be mushy. Add the nuts. Season to taste with the lemon juice, salt, and pepper. Serve immediately or keep warm for up to 20 minutes.

—DIANE MORGAN

COOKING RIGHT

Because the skin of chopped hazelnuts can come off in large pieces, skinning them results in a cleaner look and taste.

DESSERTS

Few offers are as good as this one: "Would you like some dessert?"
Whether you like to end a meal with the bracing tartness of a lemon
tart, the sweet decadence of a chocolate cheesecake, or the light
and sophisticated flavor of a pear and Champagne sorbet, you will
find a sweet in this chapter that appeals to you.

THE RECIPES

Grilled Pineapple with Butter Rum Sauce

Strawberries with Balsamic Sabayon

Pear & Champagne Sorbet

Coffee Ice Cream with Sour Cream Ganache & Toffee Chips

Lemon Tart with Walnut Crust

Cornmeal-Crusted Peach Tart

Plum Galette with Lemon Crust

Double-Crust Jumble Berry Pie

Strawberry Shortcakes

Orange-Soaked Bundt Cake

Cranberry Streusel Cake

Cream Cheese & Wild Blueberry Pound Cake

Ginger-Mascarpone Icebox Cake

Triple Chocolate Cheesecake

Chocolate Terrine with Whipped Cream & Almond Brittle

Crème Brûlée

Toasted Almond Butter Thins

Peppermint Brownies

COOKING RIGHT

You can make the sauce right on the grill or make it ahead and simply reheat it when ready to serve.

Grilled Pineapple with Butter-Rum Sauce

SERVES 8

The heat of the grill caramelizes the sugars in the pineapple, adding a toasty sweetness to this quick-to-make dessert. Serve the pineapple with some vanilla ice cream.

8 Tablespoons (1 stick) unsalted butter
1 cup lightly packed brown sugar
½ cup Meyers or other dark rum
 A pinch each of nutmeg, cinnamon, allspice
 Oil or spray oil for the grill
8 slices, 1 inch thick, very ripe fresh pineapple,
 cored if not totally soft in the center

In a small saucepan, cook the butter, sugar, rum, and spices over medium heat, stirring, until the sugar is dissolved and the butter melted. Bring to a simmer and let cook for about 10 minutes longer, stirring occasionally, until the sauce is slightly syrupy and coats the back of a spoon. Keep warm.

Heat the grill, making sure it's clean, and brush or spray it with a touch of oil so the pineapple doesn't stick. Grill the pineapple slices until warmed through and caramelized, about 10 minutes each side.

Serve immediately, in rings or chunks, with the warm sauce and ice cream, if you like.

—PARK KERR

Strawberries with Balsamic Sabayon

SERVES 8

Serve fresh strawberries with this chilled creamy sabayon sauce enhanced with balsamic vinegar. The sauce will taste complex and delicious with a really good quality aged balsamic, but it's wonderful as well when made with a more ordinary balsamic.

- 6 Tablespoons sugar
- 4 egg yolks
- 2 Tablespoons aged balsamic vinegar
- 1½ cups heavy cream, whipped to medium-stiff peaks and refrigerated
- 1 pint strawberries, rinsed if necessary and hulled
  Crisp cookies for garnish (optional)

Make the sabayon—Set aside a big bowl of ice. In a small stainless-steel bowl, whisk the sugar into the egg yolks until thoroughly combined and lightened in color. Set the bowl over a saucepan of simmering water and continue whisking the mixture until it thickens. The mixture is cooked when it's light in color and it trails off the whisk in ribbons. Do not overcook it. Remove the bowl from the heat and whisk in the balsamic vinegar. Set the bowl over the bowl of ice and continue whisking the sabayon until it's completely cooled, 5 to 10 minutes. The sabayon will stiffen as it cools. Very gently fold in the whipped cream and refrigerate the lightened sabayon for at least 2 hours before serving. It will hold overnight, but it's best served the day it's made.

Serve the sabayon draped over whole or sliced strawberries in a pretty glass dish with a garnish of crisp cookies, whole or crumbled, if you like.

—STEPHEN DURFEE

COOKING RIGHT

Because barely adorned fresh strawberries are the star here, choose plump, red berries with their dark green leaves still attached, if possible.

COOKING RIGHT

Even though the pears don't have to look pretty for this recipe, a melon baller is still an efficient tool for coring pears with the least waste.

Pear & Champagne Sorbet

YIELDS 5 CUPS

Juniper berries add depth to the otherwise sweet pear flavor, but the sorbet is also delicious without them.

1½ cups water
1½ cups sugar
¾ cup Champagne or dry white wine
5 pears, peeled, halved, cored, and cut into chunks
8 juniper berries, crushed with the back of a knife
   and tied in cheesecloth (optional)
1 Tablespoon Poire William eau de vie
1 vanilla bean
1 piece of orange zest, about 1x3 inches
   Juice from ½ lemon

In a large, heavy-based saucepan, combine the water and sugar over high heat. Stir occasionally until the sugar is dissolved and the syrup is simmering, about 5 minutes. Remove from the heat. You should have about 2 cups.

To the sugar syrup add the Champagne, pears, juniper berries, Poire William, vanilla bean, and orange zest. Simmer over medium-low heat until the pears are very tender, about 15 minutes.

Take the pan off the heat. Remove the orange zest, vanilla bean, and juniper berries, squeezing the cheesecloth. Purée the pears and liquid in a blender. Add the lemon juice. Strain the purée into a large bowl set over ice to cool. Freeze the purée in an ice-cream maker, following the manufacturer's instructions.

—FRANK MCCLELLAND

Coffee Ice Cream with Sour Cream Ganache & Toffee Chips

SERVES 4 TO 6; YIELDS ABOUT 1 CUP SAUCE

The slight tang of sour cream makes this easy sauce a standout.

6 ounces semisweet chocolate, chopped (or use chocolate chips)

⅓ cup sour cream, at room temperature

¼ teaspoon pure vanilla extract

3 to 4 Tablespoons water

1 quart coffee ice cream, slightly softened

¼ cup toffee chips

2 Tablespoons sliced almonds, toasted

Melt the chocolate in the top of a double boiler over barely simmering water, stirring frequently, until completely melted. (Or put the chocolate in a Pyrex bowl and heat in the microwave, uncovered, until melted and hot, about 1 minute on high.) Stir in the sour cream and vanilla. Continuing to stir, drizzle 3 to 4 tablespoons water into the sauce until it reaches a smooth, pourable consistency. Ladle the warm sauce on top of individual scoops of coffee ice cream and scatter with the toffee chips and almond slices.

—LAUREN GROVEMAN

COOKING AHEAD

You can make the sauce earlier in the day and reheat it either in a microwave or in a double boiler.

Lemon Tart with Walnut Crust

YIELDS ONE 9½-INCH TART; SERVES 8

Serve this luscious tart chilled or at room temperature.

  2   ounces (½ cup) chopped walnuts, toasted lightly in a dry skillet
12   Tablespoons (1½ sticks) butter, slightly softened
  2   ounces (½ cup) confectioners' sugar
  5   large eggs
7¾   ounces (1¾ cups) flour
  1   cup sugar
  ½   cup plus 2 Tablespoons fresh lemon juice (2 or 3 lemons)
  ½   cup heavy cream

Grind the walnuts to a fine grind in a food processor. Using an electric mixer with the paddle attachment, beat the butter and confectioners' sugar at high speed until light and fluffy. Add 1 of the eggs; mix to combine. Lower the speed to slow and add the flour, mixing until barely combined. Add the walnuts and continue mixing, scraping the sides of the bowl, until the dough comes together. Divide the dough. Wrap the half you'll be using in plastic and refrigerate for at least 2 hours or overnight and wrap and freeze the other for future use.

Heat the oven to 400°F. Lightly oil a 9½-inch tart pan. On a lightly floured surface, roll the dough into a round about ⅛ inch thick. Arrange it in the pan, trimming to fit. Line the crust with foil or parchment and weight with beans or pie weights. Bake until the edge is light golden brown, about 20 minutes. Carefully remove the beans and foil and bake until the bottom is dry and light brown, about another 5 minutes. Cool to room temperature.

Heat the oven to 350°F. In a medium bowl, whisk the 4 remaining eggs. Add the sugar, lemon juice and cream and whisk until just combined. Strain the mixture through a fine strainer and pour into the prepared pie crust.

Reduce the oven temperature to 325°F. Bake the tart until the filling is set, 25 to 30 minutes. Cool at room temperature. Serve at room temperature or chilled.

—DEBRA PONZEK

Cornmeal-Crusted Peach Tart

YIELDS ONE 9-INCH TART; SERVES 6 TO 8

Don't worry if the dough falls apart when you transfer it to the pan. It's easily patched, and the finished tart is meant to look rustic.

For the pastry:

12 Tablespoons (1½ sticks) unsalted butter, slightly softened

1 cup sugar

4 egg yolks

9 ounces (2 cups) flour

⅔ cup cornmeal or polenta

1 teaspoon salt

For the filling and glaze:

6 large ripe peaches, peeled and cut into ¾-inch slices (about 6 cups)

¼ cup sugar

2 Tablespoons flour

Cream

Sugar for sprinkling

COOKING RIGHT

Tossing the peaches with flour before adding to them the crust thickens the pie's juices.

Make the pastry—Cream together the butter and sugar just until fluffy. Add the egg yolks and beat until well combined. Add the flour, cornmeal, and salt and mix just until the dough comes together. Divide the dough into two pieces. Cover with plastic wrap and let rest briefly in the refrigerator.

Make the filling—Toss the peaches with the sugar. Let drain in a colander briefly and then toss with the flour.

Assemble the tart—Heat the oven to 350°F. Roll one piece of dough into an 8-inch round, fit it into a 9-inch tart pan, and press it up the sides of the pan with your fingertips. Add the peaches. Roll the remaining dough into a 9-inch round and lay it on top. Press the edges of the two pieces of dough together and flatten them against the edge of the pan; trim any excess. Brush the surface with a little cream and sprinkle with sugar. Set the tart pan on a baking sheet and bake until light golden brown, about 1 hour. Cool before removing from the pan.

—KATHLEEN STEWART

Double-Crust Jumble Berry Pie

YIELDS ONE 9-INCH DOUBLE-CRUST PIE

Since all these berries are juicy, you'll use both tapioca and cornstarch to keep the texture of the filling somewhat firm and the juices contained around the fruit. You can use these same measurements for sliced or chunked stone fruit, such as peaches, nectarines, or plums.

For the crust:

9 ounces (2 cups) all-purpose unbleached flour

¼ cup sugar

¼ teaspoon salt

8 ounces (1 cup) cold unsalted butter, cut into ½-inch cubes

¼ cup cold water

For the filling:

1 cup sugar

2 Tablespoons cornstarch

2 Tablespoons quick-cooking tapioca

¼ teaspoon salt

6 cups washed and well-dried mix of blackberries, blueberries, raspberries, and quartered strawberries

1 Tablespoon unsalted butter, cut into small pieces

Make the crust—Using the paddle attachment of a stand mixer, combine the flour, sugar, and salt. Add the butter and mix on low until the mixture is crumbly and the largest pieces of butter are no bigger than ¼ inch. (Or cut in the butter by hand using a pastry cutter.) With the mixer still on low (or tossing with a fork if making the crust by

COOK'S CHOICE

A mix of berries (with just a few strawberries) creates a delicious, summery pie. But you can also make this pie with only one type of berry or even with chunked stone fruit, such as peaches, nectarines, and plums—singly or in concert.

hand), sprinkle the water evenly over the mixture. Work the dough until it just pulls together as a shaggy mass.

Cut the dough in half and pat each piece into a flattened ball. Do not chill the dough at this point. Instead, on a lightly floured work surface, roll one piece into a circle that is at least 12 inches in diameter. Use a knife to trim any rough edges. Fold the dough in half, and with the outstretched fingers of both hands, gently lift the dough and transfer it to a 9-inch pie pan. Unfold the dough and ease it into the bottom of the pan without stretching it. Roll the remaining piece of dough into a 12-inch circle.

Make the filling—Combine the sugar, cornstarch, tapioca, and salt. Add the berries and toss until evenly coated.

Assemble the pie—Pile the berries into the dough-lined pan. Dot the surface with the butter. Use two hands to transfer the remaining dough round on top of the berries. Press the two layers of dough together to seal them and then fold the top layer over the bottom one. Flute the edges by lifting up a section of dough and pressing down on either side (see the photos above). Cut 5 or 6 slits in the top crust to let steam escape while baking. Heat the oven to 400°F while you chill the pie in the refrigerator for 15 to 20 minutes. Put the pie on a baking sheet to catch any drips and bake it for 15 minutes; reduce the oven temperature to 350°F and continue baking until the crust is golden and the juices that are bubbling through the vents are thick and glossy. Cool the pie completely to allow the filling juices to firm up, about 5 hours. Gently reheat the pie slightly before serving, if you like.

—CAROLYN WEIL

A DOUBLE CRUST NEEDS A GOOD SEAL

1 Make a strong seal by pressing the two layers of dough together before you begin to fold.

2 Create a thick, uniform edge by folding the top layer over the bottom.

3 Flute the edges by lifting up a section of dough and pressing down on either side.

COOKING RIGHT

Slits cut into the pie before baking let steam from the moist fruit escape and also let you know the pie is done by revealing thick, glossy juices.

Strawberry Shortcake
SERVES NINE

A stellar biscuit separates this from ordinary shortcake. Topped with billowy whipped cream and sweet juicy strawberries, it's truly irresistable.

For the biscuits:

13½ ounces (about 3 cups) all-purpose flour
  3 Tablespoons sugar; plus about
      3 Tablespoons for sprinkling
1½ Tablespoons baking powder
 ¾ teaspoon salt
12 Tablespoons (1½ sticks) cold unsalted
      butter, cut into small pieces
1½ cups heavy cream; plus about
      3 Tablespoons for brushing
1½ teaspoons vanilla extract

For the strawberries:

  5 cups ⅛-inch-thick strawberry slices (about 3 pints)
  1 to 3 Tablespoons sugar

For the whipped cream:

1½ cups heavy cream
  2 Tablespoons sugar
 ¾ teaspoon vanilla extract

Make the biscuits—Line a heavy baking sheet with parchment. Sift the flour, sugar, baking powder, and salt into a large bowl. Toss with a fork to combine. Cut the butter into the flour mixture with a pastry cutter or a fork until the largest pieces of butter are the size of peas. Combine the cream and vanilla in a liquid measure. Make a well in the center of the flour and pour the cream mixture into the well. Mix with a fork until the dough is evenly moistened and just combined; it should look shaggy andstill feel a little dry. Gently knead by hand 5 or 6 times to pick up any dry ingredients remaining in the bottom of the bowl and to create a loose ball.

Turn the dough out onto a lightly floured work surface and pat it into an 8-inch square, ¾ to 1 inch thick. Transfer the dough to the parchment-

COOKING AHEAD

The biscuits taste best warm (not hot) out of the oven. You can make them several hours ahead and rewarm them in a 200°F oven until warmed through with excellent results. You can slice the berries earlier in the day, but resist tossing them with the sugar until no more than a couple of hours before serving.

lined baking sheet, cover with plastic wrap, and chill for 20 minutes. Meanwhile, heat the oven to 425°F. Remove the dough from the refrigerator and trim about ¼ inch from each side to create a neat, sharp edge (a bench knife or a pastry scraper works well, or use a large chef's knife, being sure to cut straight down). Cut the dough into 9 even squares (about 2½ inches square) and spread them about 2 inches apart on the baking sheet. With a pastry brush or the back of a spoon, brush each biscuit with a thin layer of cream and sprinkle generously with sugar. Bake until the biscuits are medium golden brown on top and the bottoms are golden brown, 18 to 20 minutes.

Meanwhile, prepare the strawberries—Toss the berries with 1 tablespoon sugar and taste. If they're still tart, sprinkle with another 1 to 2 tablespoons sugar. Let sit at room temperature until the sugar dissolves and the berries begin to release their juices, at least 30 minutes but no more than 2 hours.

Whip the cream—Pour the cream into a cold mixing bowl and beat with a hand mixer until it begins to thicken. Add the sugar and vanilla extract and, using a whisk, continue to beat by hand until the cream is softly whipped or until the whisk leaves distinct marks in the cream; it should be soft and billowy but still hold its shape.

Assemble the shortcakes—While the biscuits are still warm, split them in half horizontally with a serrated knife. For each serving, set the bottom half of a biscuit on a plate. Scoop about ½ cup of the berries and their juices over the biscuit. Add a generous dollop of whipped cream and cover with the top half of the biscuit. Put a few strawberries on the top half of the biscuit before the final dollop of whipped cream and serve.

—KATHERINE EASTMAN SEELY

COOKING RIGHT

Tossing the berries in sugar not only sweetens them, but it also gets their juices flowing and softens them a bit so that they'll settle nicely into the biscuit.

Orange-Soaked Bundt Cake

SERVES 10

*This amazingly moist and delicious cake actually improves in flavor
a day or two after it's baked.*

For the cake:

10 ounces (2¼ cups) all-purpose flour; more for the pan
 2 cups sugar
1½ teaspoons baking powder
 ½ teaspoon baking soda
12 Tablespoons (1½ sticks) unsalted butter, softened; more for the pan
 ¾ cup canola or other mild-flavored oil
1½ Tablespoons finely minced lemon zest (about 2 lemons)
 1 Tablespoon vanilla extract
 ¾ cup strained fresh orange juice
 5 large eggs

For the syrup & glaze:

 ½ cup frozen orange juice concentrate, thawed
 1 Tablespoon unsalted butter, melted
 2 Tablespoons dark rum
 1 cup confectioners' sugar, divided

Heat the oven to 350°F. Butter and flour a 10-inch tube pan or 12-cup
bundt pan.

Make the cake—Sift the flour, sugar, baking powder, and soda into the
large bowl of a stand mixer fitted with the paddle attachment. Add the
butter and mix on low speed until fine crumbs form. Change to the
whisk attachment. With the machine running on medium speed, whisk in
the oil, lemon zest, vanilla extract, and orange juice. Whisk in the eggs
one at a time and then increase the speed to high and whisk the batter
until light, about 3 minutes, scraping the sides of the bowl if necessary.
Pour the batter into the prepared pan and bake until a toothpick inserted
in the cake comes out clean, 45 to 50 minutes.

Make the syrup and glaze—While the cake bakes, whisk together in a small bowl the orange juice concentrate, butter, rum, and ½ cup of the confectioners' sugar. When the cake is done, set the pan on a rack to cool for 5 minutes. With a thin skewer, poke the cake all the way through to the bottom of the pan in about 100 places. Pour ⅓ cup of the syrup over the cake and let stand for 1 hour before removing the cake from the pan. (At this point you can wrap the cake in plastic and hold for up to 3 days at room temperature; in fact, the flavor only improves.) Cover the remaining syrup with plastic and store at room temperature.

When ready to serve, whisk the remaining ½ cup confectioners' sugar into the remaining syrup. Set the cake on a rack over a baking sheet and pour the glaze over the cake. Let stand for at least 10 minutes before slicing and serving.

—KATHERINE ALFORD

COOKING RIGHT

Check the freshness of your oil before adding it to the cake batter; if it has an "off" aroma, find another bottle or risk wrecking the cake's flavor.

Cranberry Streusel Cake

SERVES 9

*Add the topping 40 minutes into baking rather than at the beginning,
when it would sink too far into the cake, or at the end, when it
wouldn't sink in at all.*

For the cake:

9 ounces (2 cups) all-purpose flour; more for the pan
1 teaspoon baking powder
½ teaspoon baking soda
½ teaspoon ground nutmeg
¼ teaspoon table salt
8 Tablespoons (1 stick) unsalted butter, well softened at room
temperature; more for the pan
1⅓ cups sugar
1 teaspoon vanilla extract
3 large eggs, at room temperature
1 cup plain, low-fat yogurt
½ cup fresh cranberries, chopped

For the streusel:

¼ cup packed light brown sugar
2 Tablespoons all-purpose flour
½ teaspoon ground cinnamon
2 Tablespoons cold unsalted butter, cut into 4 pieces
¼ cup chopped walnuts
¼ cup fresh cranberries, chopped

Stock up on packages of fresh cranberries
while they're at the peak of their season (late
fall). Freeze them to use all year long.

Make the cake—Position a rack in the middle of the oven and heat the
oven to 325°F. Lightly butter and flour a 9-inch-square baking pan. In a
medium bowl, whisk the flour, baking powder, baking soda, nutmeg,
and salt until blended. With an electric mixer, beat the butter, sugar, and
vanilla on medium speed until well blended, about 3 minutes. Reduce

To flour a pan: Spoon a generous amount of flour into the greased pan. Tilt the pan so that the flour slides all over the inside surfaces of the pan. Dump out the extra flour and give the pan a few hard knocks over the garbage can to get rid of any excess.

the speed to medium low and add the eggs one at a time, mixing until just incorporated. Using a wide rubber spatula, alternately fold the flour mixture and the yogurt into the butter mixture, beginning and ending with the flour mixture. Add the chopped cranberries with the last addition of flour. Scrape the batter into the prepared pan and spread it evenly. Tap the pan gently on the counter to release any air bubbles. Bake for 40 minutes.

Make the streusel—While the cake is baking, combine the brown sugar, flour, and cinnamon in a medium bowl. Add the butter and mix, using a fork, until the ingredients are well blended and form small crumbs. Stir in the walnuts and cranberries.

After the cake has baked for 40 minutes, sprinkle the streusel evenly over the top of the cake. Continue baking until a pick inserted in the center comes out clean, another 10 to 15 minutes. Cool in the pan on a wire rack until warm or room temperature. Cut into squares and serve.

—ABIGAIL JOHNSON DODGE

Cream Cheese & Wild Blueberry Pound Cake

YIELDS ONE 8X5-INCH LOAF

Most grocery stores carry frozen wild blueberries now. Don't let them thaw or the juices will streak the batter.

6¾ ounces (1½ cups) all-purpose unbleached flour
½ teaspoon baking powder
½ teaspoon salt
3 ounces cream cheese, at room temperature
4 ounces (½ cup) unsalted butter, slightly soft (70°F)
1½ cups sugar
4 large eggs, at room temperature
1 teaspoon pure vanilla extract
1 teaspoon grated lemon zest
1 cup wild blueberries

Heat the oven to 325°F. Spray a 8x5x3-inch loaf pan with a nonstick coating.

Whisk together the flour, baking powder, and salt until well blended. With the paddle attachment of an electric mixer, beat the cream cheese and butter until very pale and little tails have formed. Sprinkle in the sugar and beat well until slightly fluffy. Scrape the sides of the bowl well. Add the eggs one at a time, beating until blended before adding the next. With the mixer on low, add the flour, vanilla, and lemon zest, and mix until almost incorporated but not quite. Switch from the mixer to a stiff rubber spatula and mix just until the batter is well blended and smooth, scraping the bowl well. Gently fold in the berries.

Scrape the batter into the loaf pan and bake in the middle of the oven until the cake is golden brown and a toothpick comes out with just a few crumbs clinging to it when inserted in the center, 60 to 65 minutes if using fresh berries, 75 to 90 minutes if using frozen. Let the cake cool for about 15 minutes and then invert the pan and lightly tap it to release the cake. Cool completely on a rack before serving.

—CAROLYN WEIL

COOKING RIGHT

For the lightest texture, cream the butter until lots of little tails form around the beater.

Ginger-Mascarpone Icebox Cake

SERVES 12

Delicious on its own, this cake is also lovely paired with some bright-flavored fruit, such as blueberries or slices of mango or peach.

COOKING AHEAD

This cake *has* to be made ahead as it needs a good chill to firm it up.

12 ounces gingersnap crumbs, about 2¼ cups (about 40 cookies)
 5 Tablespoons unsalted butter, melted
 8 ounces cream cheese, at room temperature
 ½ cup plain low-fat yogurt
 ⅔ cup sugar; more for the pan
 ½ teaspoon vanilla extract
 ½ cup minced candied (crystallized) ginger
 1 pound mascarpone
 ⅓ cup heavy cream

Spray a 9-inch springform pan with cooking spray or grease it lightly. Dust with a little sugar and knock out any excess. Rub the gingersnap crumbs and butter together with your fingertips to combine. Sprinkle half over the bottom of the pan and pat down evenly; reserve the rest.

With an electric mixer, whip together the cream cheese, yogurt, sugar, vanilla, and candied ginger until smooth. Add the mascarpone and cream and whip until the mixture is thoroughly combined and just holds peaks. Carefully spoon half of the mascarpone cream over the crust, spreading it evenly to the edges of the pan.

Sprinkle half of the remaining crumbs over the mascarpone cream in the pan. Top with remaining mascarpone cream and finish with the remaining crumbs. Gently tap the pan on the counter to eliminate any air bubbles. Cover with plastic wrap and refrigerate overnight.

—HEATHER HO

Triple-Chocolate Cheesecake

YIELDS ONE 9-INCH CAKE; SERVES 16

*This smooth, creamy cheesecake was created
with choco-holics in mind. For the creamiest texture,
don't overwhip the filling mixture.*

For the crust:

1½ cups very finely crushed chocolate cookie
   crumbs (about 30 Nabisco® Famous
   Chocolate Wafers)

3 Tablespoons sugar

⅛ teaspoon ground cinnamon (optional)

4 Tablespoons unsalted butter, melted

For the filling:

½ cup sour cream

2 teaspoons vanilla extract

1 teaspoon instant coffee granules or espresso powder

8 ounces bittersweet chocolate, finely chopped

3 packages (8 ounces each) cream cheese, at room temperature

3 Tablespoons natural, unsweetened cocoa powder, sifted if lumpy

¼ teaspoon salt

1¼ cups sugar

3 large eggs, at room temperature

Make the crust—Heat the oven to 400°F. In a medium-sized bowl, stir
together the cookie crumbs, sugar, and cinnamon (if using) until blended.
Drizzle with the melted butter and mix until well blended and the
crumbs are evenly moist. Dump the mixture into a 9-inch springform
pan and press evenly onto the bottom and about 1 inch up the sides of
the pan (to press, use plastic wrap, a straight-sided, flat-based coffee mug,
or a tart tamper). Bake for 10 minutes and set on a wire rack to cool.
Reduce the oven temperature to 300°F.

Make the filling and bake—Mix the sour cream, vanilla, and coffee granules
in a small bowl. Set aside and stir occasionally until the coffee dissolves.

Melt the chocolate in a double boiler or in a microwave; see the sidebar
on the facing page. Stir until smooth. Set aside to cool slightly.

COOKING RIGHT

**Chop chocolate into even-size
pieces** for less chance of scorching
during melting. Use a large chef's
knife and bear down with both
hands. Working on parchment paper
makes cleaning easier.

In a stand mixer fitted with the paddle attachment, beat the cream cheese, cocoa powder, and salt until very smooth and fluffy, scraping down the sides of the bowl and paddle frequently (and with each subsequent addition). Add the sugar and continue beating until well blended and smooth. Scrape the cooled chocolate into the bowl; beat until blended. Beat in the sour cream mixture until well blended. Add the eggs, one at a time, and beat until just blended. (Don't overbeat the filling once the eggs have been added or the cheesecake will puff too much.) Pour the filling over the cooled crust, spread evenly, and smooth the top. Bake at 300°F until the center barely jiggles when nudged, 50 to 60 minutes. The cake will be slightly puffed, with a few little cracks around the edge. Let cool to room temperature on a rack and then refrigerate until well chilled, at least a few hours, or overnight for the best texture and flavor.

To serve—Unclasp the pan's ring, remove it, and run a long, thin metal spatula under the bottom crust. Carefully slide the cake onto a flat serving plate. Run a thin knife under hot water, wipe it dry, and cut the cake into slices, heating and wiping the knife as needed.

—ABIGAIL JOHNSON DODGE

COOKING AHEAD

This cake freezes really well. Put the unmolded cake in the freezer, uncovered, until the top is cold and firm, and then wrap it in two layers of plastic and one layer of foil. Defrost the cake in the refrigerator for a day before unmolding and serving it.

MELTING CHOCOLATE IN THE MICROWAVE

Microwaves vary greatly, so adjust the timing to suit your machine.

- Put finely chopped chocolate in a wide, shallow bowl and heat on high or medium-high until it just starts to melt, about a minute.

- Give the chocolate a good stir and microwave again until almost completely melted, 15 to 30 seconds.

- Remove and stir the chocolate until completely melted.

Almond Brittle
YIELDS ABOUT 1¼ POUNDS

2½ cups sugar

¾ cup water

2 Tablespoons unsalted butter

5 ounces (1 cup) whole almonds, toasted, cooled, and coarsely chopped

Grease a rimmed baking sheet with oil. Put the sugar in a medium saucepan without catching any crystals on the walls of the pan. Add the water, pouring it around the walls to rinse down any sugar that might be there. Let the mixture sit for 1 minute (don't stir) so that the water infiltrates the sugar.

Over high heat, boil the mixture without stirring until it turns very light amber, about 10 minutes. (Test the color of the caramel by dripping a bit onto a white plate.) Remove from the heat and stir in the butter with a wooden spoon just until melted and evenly blended. Stir in the nuts and then immediately pour the mixture across the prepared baking sheet. Let cool.

Break the brittle into manageable pieces and then chop half of it for the terrine (save the rest for snacking). The brittle can be stored in an airtight container for up to a week.

Chocolate Terrine with Whipped Cream & Almond Brittle
SERVES 12

A crunchy almond brittle exaggerates the terrine's silky texture.

8 ounces good-quality semisweet chocolate, coarsely chopped

12 Tablespoons (1½ sticks) unsalted butter, cut into 12 pieces; more for the pan

¾ cup sugar

½ cup brewed coffee (fresh or leftover)

4 large eggs, beaten
Almond Brittle (see the recipe at left)

1 cup heavy cream

COOKING AHEAD

You can make the terrine a day ahead; wrap it well and keep it refrigerated. The brittle can be stored for a week in an airtight container.

Position an oven rack in the lower middle of the oven and heat the oven to 350°F. Grease an 8x5-inch loaf pan and line it with heavy-duty foil, making sure not to puncture it.

Fill a medium saucepan halfway with water and bring the water to a simmer. Put the chocolate and butter in a stainless-steel bowl large enough to fit over the pan without dipping into the water. Set the bowl over the simmering water, stirring the chocolate and butter with a whisk until melted and blended. Add the sugar and coffee, slowly stirring to dissolve the sugar. Continue cooking until the mixture is hot to the touch and the sugar is dissolved. Remove the bowl from the heat and whisk in the beaten eggs. Pour the chocolate mixture into the lined loaf pan.

Set a large baking dish on the oven rack. Set the loaf pan in the center of the baking dish and surround it with 1 inch of very hot water. Bake until the chocolate has begun to lose its shine, doesn't shimmy when jostled, and just begins to puff slightly around the edges, 40 to 50 minutes. Remove the terrine from the oven and cool on a rack to room temperature. Cover with plastic wrap and chill in the refrigerator for at least 4 hours or overnight.

Meanwhile, make the almond brittle (See the recipe on the facing page.)

Lift the terrine out of the loaf pan, using the foil as a sling. Turn it over onto a platter or cutting board and peel off the foil. Using a knife that has been dipped in hot water and wiped dry, cut the terrine into ½-inch slices. (For even slices, trim off the ends of the loaf first.)

In a chilled medium stainless-steel bowl, beat the heavy cream with a whisk or an electric mixer at medium-high speed until it holds soft peaks when the beaters are lifted. Serve each slice of the terrine with a dollop of the whipped cream and a tablespoon-size sprinkling of the chopped almond brittle.

—GALE GAND

THE RIGHT LOOK FOR CARAMEL

Too light. This scant color won't give you much flavor, just sweetness; keep cooking.

Just right. A deep amber means a sweet but toasty flavor. Take it off the heat now.

Too dark. Caramel cooked this far will taste too bitter. Start over.

Slowly drizzle the white chocolate in an inexact but evenly distributed pattern. Drag a thin skewer or toothpick through the glazes in alternating directions to create a marbled look.

Peppermint Brownies

YIELDS ABOUT 30 BROWNIES

These brownies only get better after a couple of days, as their texture gets fudgier and their flavor richer. Peppermint extract is available in grocery stores or by mail order.

20 Tablespoons (2½ sticks) unsalted butter; more for greasing the pan
10 ounces unsweetened chocolate
2 teaspoons peppermint tea leaves (about 2 tea bags)
2 cups sugar
4 large eggs
2 teaspoons peppermint extract
¼ teaspoon kosher salt
4½ ounces (1 cup) all-purpose flour
2 ounces semisweet chocolate
2 Tablespoons light corn syrup
2 ounces white chocolate

Center a rack in the oven and heat the oven to 350°F. Butter the bottom and sides of a 9x13-inch baking pan, line it with parchment (the paper should extend at least an inch above the long sides to act as handles for getting the brownies out), and butter the paper.

Put about 2 inches of water in a small pot and heat to a gentle simmer. In a heatproof bowl set over the water, melt 8 ounces of the butter and 8 ounces of the unsweetened chocolate. Be sure that the water is hot but not boiling and that it doesn't touch the bottom of the bowl. Stir occasionally with a heatproof spatula until the mixture is completely melted and uniform, 6 to 7 minutes. Turn off the heat, but leave the bowl over the water.

In a food processor, finely grind the peppermint leaves with the sugar. In a medium bowl, whisk together the eggs, peppermint extract, salt, and peppermint sugar until just combined. Whisk in the melted chocolate mixture (reserve the pot of water for later). Slowly add the flour, gently folding it in with a spatula, until incorporated. Spread the batter into the

prepared pan and bake until a pick inserted into the center comes out almost clean (a few bits of batter should cling to the pick), 35 to 40 minutes. Put the pan on a rack to cool to room temperature, about 2 hours. Lift the paper lining to pull the brownies out of the pan. Peel the paper off the brownies and put them on a cutting board.

To make the glaze, bring the pot of water back to a gentle simmer. Set a heatproof bowl over the pot and add the semisweet chocolate, corn syrup, and the remaining 2 ounces each butter and unsweetened chocolate. Stir frequently with a heatproof spatula until the mixture is melted and smooth; set aside. Put the white chocolate in a separate heatproof bowl and set it over the water. Stir frequently until it's melted and smooth; remove it from the heat.

Spread the chocolate glaze over the cooled brownies in an even layer using a spatula. Drizzle the white chocolate over the glaze in lines. Use a toothpick or a wooden skewer to drag the white chocolate into the glaze (as shown in the bottom photo on the facing page). Lift the cutting board and firmly tap it on the counter to settle the glaze.

Refrigerate until the glaze is set, at least 20 minutes and up to 12 hours. Cut into thirty bars, about 2 inches square (a knife rinsed in hot water and then dried will cut more cleanly than a cold knife). Keep well covered and serve at room temperature.

—GREG CASE

Bios

FINE COOKING STAFF CONTRIBUTOR BIOS:

Jennifer Armentrout is *Fine Cooking's* Test Kitchen Supervisor and Recipe Developer (recipes on pp. 48, 160).

Martha Holmberg is *Fine Cooking's* Publisher and Editor-In-Chief (recipes on pp. 20, 22, 33, 50, 140, 154).

Kim Landi is an editorial assistant at *Fine Cooking* (recipe on p. 142).

Susie Middleton is an editor at *Fine Cooking* (recipes on pp. 36, 58, 178, 183, 184, 187, 188, 190).

Joanne McAllister Smart, a former editor at *Fine Cooking,* co-authored the award-winning cookbook *Bistro Cooking at Home* with Gordon Hamersley, and is currently writing a book on Italian cooking with New York chef, Scott Conant (recipe on p. 61).

CONTRIBUTOR BIOS:

Barbara Witt is the author of *The Weekend Chef* (Simon & Schuster, 2003) (recipe on p. 6).

Amanda Hesser is the food editor at *The New York Times* magazine, and the author of *The Cook and the Gardener* (2000) and *Cooking for Mr. Latte: A Food Lover's Courtship, with Recipes* (both from W.W. Norton & Company) (recipe on p. 8).

Tasha DeSerio, a former cook at Chez Panisse, is a cooking teacher and writer (recipes on pp. 14, 171).

Craig Stoll is the chef and co-owner of Delfina restaurant in San Francisco (recipe on p. 9).

John Ash, a highly regarded, nationally known food and wine educator, is also the author of *John Ash: Cooking One-on-One: Lessons from a Master Teacher* (Clarkson Potter, 2004) (recipes on pp. 10, 157, 162).

Paula LeDuc owns Paula LeDuc Fine Catering, based in Emeryville, California. Her company caters events ranging from intimate dinners to the opening night at the San Francisco Opera (recipes on pp. 11–12).

Lisa Hanauer is a recovered chef/restaurateur living in Oakland, CA, where she and her daughter, Gemma, never miss a farmer's market (recipes on pp. 13, 182).

Molly Stevens is the author of *All About Braising*; co-author of *One Potato, Two Potato*; co-editor of the *Best American Recipe Series*; contributing editor to *Fine Cooking*, and a traveling cooking instructor (recipes on pp. 16, 18, 29, 35, 42, 67, 68, 74, 81, 116, 126, 156, 177, 180).

Roy Finamore and Molly Stevens cooked their way through 1,500 pounds of potatoes while writing their book, *One Potato, Two Potato* (Houghton Mifflin, 2001) (recipe on p. 177).

Bill Briwa is a chef-instructor at the Culinary Institute of America at Greystone in St. Helena, California (recipe on p. 17).

Tony Rosenfield is a former editor at *Fine Cooking* magazine (recipes on pp. 19, 64, 73, 92, 125, 168, 170).

Sam Hayward is the chef and co-owner of Fore Street Restaurant in Portland, Maine (recipe on p. 23).

Alison Edwards is one of the founding farmers of *Dirty Girl Produce* and runs *The Green Table*, an organic catering company, both in Santa Cruz, CA (recipe on p. 26).

Georgeanne Brennan is an award-winning cookbook author and journalist who divides her time between California and Provence. She can be reached at www.georgeannebrennan.com (recipe on p. 27).

Seen Lippert is the executive chef at Across the Street restaurant in Manhattan (recipes on pp. 28, 66).

Alice Waters is the founder and proprietor of Chez Panisse in Berkeley, California (recipe on p. 30).

Joanne Weir is the host of PBS's *Weir Cooking in the City*, and the author of its companion book. Her previous book, *Joanne Weir's More Cooking in the Wine Country* (Simon & Schuster, 2001) was nominated for a James Beard Award (recipes on pp. 31, 37, 43, 59, 85, 94, 103).

Alan Tangren is the head of the pastry department at Chez Panisse (recipes on pp. 32, 173).

David Page is the chef and owner of Home Restaurant in New York City. He owns Shinn Vineyards in Mattituck, NY, with his wife, Barbara Shinn (recipe on p. 34).

Caprial Pence is co-owner of Caprial's Bistro in Portland, Oregon, and the host of PBS's television show, *Cooking with Caprial* (recipe on p. 38).

Abigail Johnson Dodge conducts classes and seminars at cooking schools around the country, appears regularly on TV and radio, and is the author of four popular cookbooks, *Kids Baking, Williams-Sonoma Dessert, The Kid's Cookbook, and Great Fruit Desserts* (recipes on pp. 40, 102, 202, 210, 214).

Paul Bertolli is the chef/co-owner of Oliveto Restaurant in Berkeley, CA, and a contributing editor to *Fine Cooking* (recipes on pp. 41, 113, 172).

Leslie Revsin was the first woman chef at the Waldorf. Her latest cookbook is *Come for Dinner: Memorable Meals to Share with Friends* (Wiley, 2003) (recipes on pp. 44, 109, 114).

Eva Katz is a freelance writer and recipe developer in Boston (recipes on pp. 52, 143, 164).

Eve Felder, a former chef at *Chez Panisse*, is the Associate Dean for Culinary Curriculum at the Culinary Institute of America. Her recipes have been featured in numerous books and magazines (recipe on pp. 54).

David Tanis is a chef and author who cooks and lives in Santa Fe, New Mexico (recipes on pp. 56, 152).

Rosina Tinari Wilson is a food consultant, teacher, and writer in Kensington, California. The author of *Seafood, Pasta & Noodles* (Ten Speed Press, 1995), she is a contributing editor to *Fine Cooking* (recipe on p. 60).

Pam Anderson is a food columnist for *USA Weekend*, contributing editor to *Fine Cooking*, and author of *The Perfect Recipe* (Houghton Mifflin, 2001) (recipes on pp. 49, 89, 90, 120, 147).

Ris Lacoste is the award-wining executive chef of 1789 Restaurant in Washington, D.C. Her website is www.1789restaurant.com (recipe on p. 70).

Daphne Zepos is a former chef, a board member of the American Cheese Society, and a cheese consultant (recipe on p. 69).

Mary Pult is the chef and Rebecca Fasten is the sous-chef at the Liberty Café in San Francisco (recipe on p. 72).

Clifford A. Wright won the James Beard Cookbook of the Year award in 2000 for *A Mediterranean Feast* (Morrow, 1999) (recipe on p. 75).

Arlene Jacobs is the former executive chef at Lot 61 and Bungalow 8 in New York, and is currently Chef/Instructor at The French Culinary Institute, as well as a freelance writer (recipes on pp. 78, 138, 174).

Paula Wolfert is the author of *Mediterranean Grains & Greens* (Harper Collins 1998) and *The Slow Mediterranean Kitchen* (Wiley, 2003) (recipe on p. 76).

Alan Tardi is a veteran of some great New York restaurants such as Chanteurelle, Lafayette, LeMadri, and Fellonico, where he was the chef and owner. He currently lives in Italy (recipes on pp. 79, 80).

Elizabeth Terry co-owns Elizabeth on 37th in Savannah, Georgia, and is devoted to classic Southern cooking (recipe on p. 84).

Leona Dalavia Scott enjoys cooking tandoori chicken and other Indian specialties with her family in Bedford, TX. Recently married to a Louisiana native, she looks forward to fusing Indian and Cajun cuisine (recipe on p. 87).

Maryellen Driscoll is *Fine Cooking*'s editor at large. She raises chickens in upstate New York (recipe on p. 88).

Grillmaster Steven Raichlen is an award-winning author, journalist, cooking teacher, and TV host. His best-selling *Barbecue Bible* cookbook series and his *Barbecue University* TV show on PBS have virtually reinvented American barbecue (recipe on p. 95).

After working for *Chez Pannise*, Mima Lecoq founded Carried Away Foods, where she and her husband, Tom McNary, prepare restaurant-quality food for both take-out and in-store dining using primarily organic, locally grown ingredients (recipe on p. 96).

Stephen Pyles was the founding chef-owner of Star-Canyon in Dallas. Currently, he's teaching and consulting (recipe on pp. 98).

Robert Wemischner teaches professional baking in Los Angeles and is the author of three books; most recently, *Cooking with Tea* (Periplus Editions, 2000) (recipe on p. 97).

Hiroko Shimbo is the author of *The Japanese Kitchen* (Harvard Common Press, 2000) (recipe on p. 100).

Jennifer Bushman is the founder of Nothing To It! Cooking School in Reno, NV (recipes on pp. 101, 139).

Tony Mantuano is the chef at Tuttaposto in Chicago, which he and his wife Cathy own along with Mangia Trattoria, in Kenosha, Wisconsin (recipe on p. 106).

Katherine Alford, former director of instruction at Peter Kump's Cooking School, is opening her own cooking school in New York City (recipes on pp. 107, 208).

Brian Streeter is the chef at Cakebread Cellars in Rutherford, CA (recipes on pp. 108, 127).

Norman Van Aken, founder of New World Cuisine, is a forerunner of the culinary fusion movement, and he is the author of four cookbooks: *Feast of Sunlight* (1988), *The Exotic Fruit Book* (1995), *Norman's New World Cuisine* (1997), and *New World Kitchen* (2003) (recipes on pp. 110, 145).

Lucia Watson, a James Beard award nominee, has been the chef at Lucia's Restaurant in Minneapolis for 19 years, and Beth Dooley is a food writer based there. The two collaborated on *Savoring the Seasons of the Northern Heartland* (Knopf, 1994) (recipes on pp. 118, 191).

Bruce Aidells co-wrote *The Complete Meat Cookbook* with Dennis Kelly. He's also the owner and founder of Aidells Sausage Company (recipe on p. 119).

Anne Willan is the founder of La Varenne Cooking School and the author of many award-winning cookbooks. Her most recent work is *The Good Cook* (Stewart, Tabori and Chang, 2004) (recipe on p. 122).

Steve Johnson is the chef-owner of The Blue Room in Cambridge, MA (recipes on pp. 124, 130, 136).

Josh Eisen lives with his wife and son in New York City, where he teaches and writes about wine and food (recipe on p. 128).

Isabelle Alexandre is the chef de cuisine at Pastis restaurant in San Francisco (recipe on p. 134).

Perla Meyers is the author of many cookbooks, including the forthcoming, *Ask Perla: The 1000 Questions You Had in Cooking School and Never Got to Ask* (recipes on pp. 135, 165).

Mai Pham is chef/owner of Lemon Grass Restaurant and Lemon Grass Cafes in Sacramento, California. She is the author of *The Best of Vietnamese & Thai Cooking* (Prima Publishing, 1996) (recipe on p. 144).

Lauren Groveman is the author of *The I Love to Cook Book* (Clarkson N. Potter, 2004) (recipes on pp. 146, 199).

Elizabeth A. Karmel is the creator of GirlsattheGrill.com. (recipe on p. 148).

Gary Danko is the chef-owner of Restaurant Gary Danko in San Francisco (recipe on p. 149).

Debra Ponzek is chef and proprietor of *Aux Delices*, a gourmet prepared food shop with full-service catering with locations in Greenwich, Riverside, and Darien, CT. She is also the author of *The Summer House Cookbook* (Clarkson N. Potter, 2003) (recipes on pp. 153, 200).

Jim Peyton has written three Mexican cookbooks, including *La Cocina de la Frontera* and *New Cooking from Old Mexico* (recipe on p. 158).

Joyce Goldstein is a restaurant and food consultant as well as the author of three cookbooks: *Solo Suppers, Saffron Shores,* and *Italian Slow and Savory* (all Chronicle, 2003, 2002, 2004 respectively) (recipe on p. 163).

Amanda Cushman is a chef, cooking teacher, and food writer who lives in New York City (recipe on p. 159).

Robert Carter is the chef at the Peninsula Grill at the Planter's Inn in Charleston, South Carolina (recipe on p. 169).

Diane Morgan is the author of *The Thanksgiving Table: Recipes & Ideas to Create Your Own Holiday Tradition* (Chronicle, 2001) (recipes on pp. 176, 193).

Karen and Ken Baker are the chef-owners of Magnolia Grill in Durham, NC, and the authors of *Not Afraid of Flavor: Recipes from Magnolia Grill* (recipe on p. 181).

French-born **Hubert Keller** is co-owner and visionary of *Fleur De Lys Restaurant* in San Francisco (recipe on p. 186).

Chef **Gordon Hamersly** and his wife, Fiona, own Hamersley's Bistro in Boston (recipe on p. 189).

Susan Goss is the chef-owner of Zinfandel restaurant in Chicago (recipe on p. 192).

Carolyn Weil has spent over 30 years in the food industry in California as a baker, teacher, and writer. Her latest book is *Pie and Tart* (Free Press, 2003) (recipes on pp. 205, 212).

W. Park Kerr, founder of the El Paso Chile Company, is the author of five cookbooks, including the series called *Beans, Chiles, and Tortillas* from William Morrow (recipe on p. 196).

Joanne Chang is the pastry chef at Payard Pâtesserie in New York (recipes on pp. 218, 219).

Frank McClelland is the chef/owner of L'Espalier in Boston (recipe on p. 198).

Stephen Durfee is the pastry chef at The French Laundry in Yountville, California (recipe on p. 197).

Kathleen Stewart runs the Downtown Bakery in Healdsburg, CA (recipe on p. 201).

Heather Ho was a graduate of The Culinary Institute of America and worked as a pastry chef in many great restaurants in San Francisco and New York (recipe on p. 213).

Katherine Eastman Seeley is a pastry chef and food writer (recipe on p. 206).

Gale Gand is the executive pastry chef and partner of Tru in Chicago (recipe on p. 216).

Greg Case is the pastry chef and owner of G. Case Baking, a retail and wholesale bakery in Boston, and the author of the forthcoming *One Cake, 100 Desserts* (William Morrow, 2006) (recipe on p. 220).

Index